BILL CLIFTON

MUSIC IN AMERICAN LIFE

*A list of books in the series appears
at the end of this book.*

BILL CLIFTON

America's Bluegrass
Ambassador to the World

BILL C. MALONE

UNIVERSITY OF ILLINOIS PRESS

Urbana, Chicago, and Springfield

Frontispiece: Photo of Bill Clifton with guitar on Station
WMBG, Williamsburg, Virginia. (Courtesy of Bill Clifton)

Library of Congress Cataloging-in-Publication Data
Names: Malone, Bill C.
Title: Bill Clifton : America's bluegrass ambassador to the world
     / Bill C. Malone.
Description: Urbana : University of Illinois Press, [2016] |
     Series: Music in American life | Includes bibliographical
     references and index.
Identifiers: LCCN 2016015396| ISBN 9780252040535
     (hardcover : alk. paper) | ISBN 9780252082009 (pbk. : alk.
     paper)
Subjects: LCSH: Clifton, Bill. | Bluegrass musicians—United
     States—Biography.
Classification: LCC ML420.C568 M35 2016 |
     DDC 782.421642092—dc23
     LC record available at https://lccn.loc.gov/2016015396

I wish to dedicate this book to Judith "Judy" McCulloh, in loving remembrance of our friendship and her unfailing support for roots music scholarship in the United States.

Judy McCulloh and Bill C. Malone at a Carter Family Conference in London, 2001. Courtesy of the photographer, Bobbie Malone

CONTENTS

ACKNOWLEDGMENTS

This is not an "authorized" biography. Bill Clifton neither financed its production nor read it in manuscript. Except for admonitions that I should "tell it like it is," he has not tried to shape the direction or tone of my remarks. Consequently, there are places where he will disagree with my conclusions. He has, however, been extremely generous in providing support, through in-person conversations and interviews, numerous telephone calls and emails, and through contact information he has provided for family, friends, and musical associates.

In addition to Bill, I wish to acknowledge the support of other family members: his wife, Tineke, his sisters Mary Lynn Brett, Fifi Peck, Ann Hoffman, and Martha Sadler, and four of his children, Charles "Tad" Marburg, Chandler Marburg, Flory Gout, and Laurel Marburg.

I am also grateful to Hamilton "Hap" Hackney, Bill's childhood and lifelong friend, and to a slate of business and musical friends who provided their recollections of him or, in the case of Nathan Gibson, wrote about his crucial affiliation with the Starday label. In addition to Gibson, the United States contributors include David Freeman, Dennis Cash, Peter Kuykendall, Tom Gray, Tom Morgan, Eddie Adcock, Jimmy Gaudreau, Fred Bartenstein, and Ronald Cohen. I did not talk to Neil Rosenberg, Joe Ross, or Richard Spottswood, but their contributions are apparent in the manuscript.

Outside the United States, my indebtedness extends to a remarkable group of people who played major roles in Bill Clifton's international career, and who have been extremely helpful to me. These include: in Germany, Richard Weize; in England, Rick Townend, Robert Ronald, John Atkins, Tony Russell, Jim Marshall, Dave Barnes, and Michael Paris; in Switzerland, Jean-Blaise Rochat; in New Zealand, Paul Trenwith; in Japan, Sam "Watanabe" Inoue; and in Holland, Rienk Janssen. Janssen's help has been immeasurable, both in his personal emails and in the wonderful notes he wrote for the book that accompanied Bill's magisterial Bear Family box collection, *From Poor Valley to the World*.

Of course, I wish to recall the music and memory of Mike Seeger, who was a frequent collaborator with Bill Clifton in the documentation and preservation of American old-time music, and who supplied me with many anecdotes about their relationship. And, as always, I wish to acknowledge the unselfish love and support of my wife, Bobbie, who read all of the chapters and provided the tough criticism I needed. I hope that our collaboration and partnership will endure for many years to come.

BILL CLIFTON

INTRODUCTION

This journey into the life and music of Bill Clifton began back in the mid-1950s with my search for what I thought was "real" country music. I despaired of the music's future, and of its gradual loss of identity. These anxieties arose in the wake of rock and roll's emergence and of the stylistic dilutions wrought by country pop. So when I heard any recording that was marked by an unapologetic display of country instrumentation—fiddle, steel guitar, five-string banjo—or by a distinctive rural vocal sound, I embraced it. George Jones had come along just a little earlier, with his rock-ribbed country vocal style, and I was thrilled to learn that Bluegrass music, for example, with its high, hard harmonies and bright acoustic instrumental sound, was flourishing artistically, if not economically. With songs like "White Dove" and "Gathering Flowers for the Master's Bouquet," the Stanley Brothers (Carter and Ralph) had reassured me that the old-time lonesome sound was still very much alive.

Actually, Bill Clifton did *not* have a hard-edged rural voice. He sang with a smooth, well-articulated, and easily understood style. He always seemed to find outstanding musical accompanists, too, and I particularly liked the twin fiddling that could sometimes be heard on his recordings. Above all, though, I liked his choice of songs. We seemed to have similar tastes in music and, like me, Bill loved to find and preserve old story songs, like "Blue Ridge Mountain Blues" and "The Mail Carrier's Warning," or sentimental tunes such as "My Old Pal of Yesterday." Bill's self-description as a "song carrier" would also fit me, and as I searched for old songs, I was particularly pleased when I came across the paperback collection he had compiled in 1955, *150 Old-Time, Folk, and Gospel Songs*. As Fred Bartenstein has argued, this little book exerted an influence among bluegrass and old-time country fans that is somewhat comparable to that wrought earlier by the Harry Smith collection on urban folk music enthusiasts.

Through this book, his album liner notes, and publications such as *Country Song Roundup* magazine, I gradually began to gather a few details concerning Bill's life. My admiration for his music began to be accompanied by bemusement about his personal history. First of all, I found that his real name was William Marburg. Immediately, I wondered if he could be Jewish. After all, I was beginning to learn that a significant number of Jewish people, such as John Cohen, Tom Paley, Jack Elliott, and Ralph Rinzler, had embraced bluegrass and old-time music. And soon I began to hear about "Jewgrass," the name given to the bluegrass music played by Jewish musicians at Washington Square and other sites in New York City. No, Bill Clifton wasn't Jewish, but he wasn't your typical "hillbilly" either. Over the years, I learned that he was a graduate of the University of Virginia, had earned an MBA from that institution, had worked as a stockbroker, had served in the Marine Corps, lived for about fifteen years in England, and had been in the Peace Corps in the Philippines. During these remarkably varied years, Bill built a successful and influential music career as well, while also managing to meet and become warm close friends with people like Woody Guthrie and A. P. Carter.

Bill's professional music heyday came at the end of the 1950s and in the early 1960s when he was recording for Mercury and Starday in Nashville. He moved to England in 1963, and I heard about him only sporadically in the years that followed. I continued to wear out his LPs, however, and to sing such songs as "Mary Dear," which I made sure to include when, in 1981, I organized, edited, and annotated the *Smithsonian Collection of Classic Country Music*. I must confess, though, that in my writings about country music during those years, I did not always honor Bill's legacy as well as I should have. In talking about his groundbreaking festival at Luray, Virginia, I mistakenly, on more than one occasion, gave the date as 1962! Thankfully, that mistake and others can be corrected in this biography.

By the time the *Smithsonian Collection* appeared, I had been teaching history at Tulane University in New Orleans for about ten years and was fronting a bluegrass band called the Hill Country Ramblers (named, rather incongruously, in honor of the Texas hill country, where I'd previously taught at Southwest Texas State University in San Marcos—now Texas State University). I had managed to attract some of the finest musicians in South Louisiana, including Eleanor Ellis, our bass player, who has since become a highly regarded blues singer and guitarist in Baltimore. Most of our performances were made at a little honky-tonk in Gretna, Louisiana, called Gurley's Bar and Grill, and at occasional festivals in that state and in Mississippi and Texas. But in 1976 another member of the Ramblers, Jim Huey—now known as "Dr. Dobro," because of the extracurricular work that he's become famous for apart from his work in Cincinnati as a physician at the veterans' hospital—came up with an exciting option for us. He contacted his musician friend, Jim Tanner, who lived in the Washington, D.C., area, and managed to secure a couple of gigs for us in Maryland, at the Red Fox Inn in Bethesda and at the Indian Springs festival sponsored by *Bluegrass Unlimited* magazine at Hagerstown.[1] Shortly before the trip, we learned that our banjo player, Joe Wilson, could not get off work. But Pat Flory, our lead guitar player, saved the day by saying, "Well, my young friend in New York City might be able to come down and play with us." The "friend" was Bela Fleck, then only about eighteen years old, but already a highly accomplished musician.[2] He has since become one of the most famous five-string banjo players in the world.

Now up to more than full strength through the addition of Bela, we showed up at the Red Fox Inn to find that we were sharing the stage with some of the greatest talent in bluegrass and old-time music. Bill Clifton was back in the United States and, along with Red Rector and Mike Seeger, was beginning an extended engagement at the club. Red Rector was a superb mandolin player with about forty years of professional experience, and Mike Seeger, of course, was the half-brother of Pete and a master musician of remarkable versatility. To our surprise and delight, we were opening for the man whose music I had so long adored! During our brief stay in Bethesda, I talked to Bill at length and explored with him the idea of an article that might appear in *Bluegrass Unlimited*. He was highly receptive to the idea and invited me to visit his father's farm near Baltimore.[3]

When I saw Selsed—his parents' home—I then realized how wealthy and privileged his past had been. Selsed was like an English country estate. I had a lengthy, fact-filled interview with Bill, more than enough information to buttress an authoritative essay.

I returned to New Orleans. Shortly after I returned, I received a telephone call from my first wife, Ann, who was in Austin preparing for her doctoral exams in history. She told me that she wasn't coming back and had already filed for divorce. While I can't blame the separation and divorce as the sole reasons for my inaction, I never did write an article on Bill Clifton. And I always wondered what Bill thought about my dereliction. I'm sure that he could have used the publicity/exposure as he sought to rejuvenate his American career.

The years rolled by, and my guilt never dissipated. I had no more contact with Bill until 2002, when I attended and participated in a Carter Family Conference in London, sponsored by Gary McDowell and the Institute of United States Studies at the University of London. I was one of several scholars, including Neil Rosenberg and Nolan Porterfield, who presented papers on the Carter Family legacy, while Bill Clifton led a panel discussion and talked about his intimate relationship with A. P. Carter. Bill was very friendly and made no mention of the incidents and failed promises of 1976. On the other hand, I did make contact with Mike Seeger and began the process that eventually led to my biography, *Music from the True Vine: Mike Seeger's Life and Musical Journey*. Bill Clifton was very helpful to me in the preparation of Seeger's biography, but I did not physically meet with him again until 2009, when we attended a memorial service for Mike in Bethesda, Maryland. Our meeting was cordial and pleasant, and our conversation, on the whole, was concerned with good and pleasant memories of Mike. Again, no mention was made of my promised and unfinished essay.

A few years after the publication of *Music from the True Vine*, I received a Facebook message from Dennis Cash, a bluegrass gospel musician, a Bill Clifton fan, and a Carter Family enthusiast. He told me that in a recent visit with Bill he had urged him to write his autobiography. And Bill Clifton had said to Dennis, "If anyone writes my biography, it should be Bill C. Malone." So, armed with this reassurance, I contacted Bill and embarked on this biographical project, hoping that I could do justice to him as a person and to the role he has played as an international ambassador for American roots music.[4]

Intensive research has not dimmed my affection for Bill's music or my regard for him as a human being. But I have become increasingly conscious of the complexities that I only dimly perceived in him almost sixty years ago. He was a man of comfortable and privileged origins who found beauty in the music of working-class people, and made it his mission to introduce it to the world. He was a man with advanced business training who was uncomfortable with money and who too often made irrational decisions concerning its use, and a man who loved and sang about the values of home and family, but who nevertheless often had strained relations with his own children and wives. His relationship with his father was a troubled one, and he never truly achieved the independence from him that he had always sought. Like many of us who have found comfort in old-time music, Bill clothed his subject in the vestments of romance and imagined a world far different from the insincere and strife-ridden world we inhabit. The little old log cabin, with the grapevine 'round the door—a powerful element in Bill's music, and a central defining motif of bluegrass and old-time country music—stands in our collective memory as a refuge from modernism, even though the modern forces of radio, recording, television, and electrical transmission have made it possible to hear and preserve such music. Bill actually inhabited both worlds simultaneously and devoted himself to playing and promoting what he found authentic, remarkable, and enduring in old-time music.

This book, then, is a tribute to Bill as well as a fulfillment of the previously mentioned debt. I cannot resurrect Bill's career, but I hope I can help to assure his memory and legacy.

1

DISCOVERING COUNTRY MUSIC, 1931–1949

William Augustus Marburg, known to the bluegrass music world as Bill Clifton, was born on Easter Sunday, April 5, 1931, in Riderwood, Maryland, an affluent suburb of Baltimore.[1] His four older, adoring sisters—Mary Lynn, Frances, Martha, and Ann—probably thought of him as a gift from the Easter Bunny. One of his sisters, Martha, who was familiar only with doll babies made from rags or plastic, enthusiastically said, "Good. Now we have a real skin baby," a baby that could smile, gurgle, and wet his diaper. The Marburg sisters doted on their baby brother Billy and soon learned that he was not only special but was also different. He proved to be, in fact, a maverick, an atypical Marburg. No one understood this more than his father, Grainger. The relationship between Bill and his father can best be described as complex and complicated. Grainger was initially delighted to finally have a son. According to Bill's eldest sister, Mary Lynn (Mimi), "Dad thought it was another girl until he was finally invited into their bedroom and actually saw his son for the first time. He was so happy that he actually jumped with joy!" But Bill never completely lived up to his father's expectations. He did not become a businessman (or at least not for long). He was not fond of guns, hunting, or many of the pursuits expected of a man's man—although he did later serve in the United States Marines. And he embraced a career in country music, which was decidedly embarrassing to his dad, if not the whole family.

To be sure, it would have been hard for any son to live up to the Marburg standards. They were one of Baltimore's leading families, and one in which men were expected to play prescribed manly roles. Their contributions to American life began in 1830, when the first William A. Marburg, Bill's great-grandfather, arrived in the United States from Nassau, Germany. By 1851 he had established a business, manufacturing cigars, which was the source of the family's economic power and social leadership. He and five of his sons later organized the Marburg Brothers Company, which became one of the leading producers of smoking tobacco in the United States. By the time the family sold its interests to the American Tobacco Company in 1891, the Marburgs had achieved distinction in the realms of art, education, politics, and community betterment. Bill's grandfather, Theodore (1862–1942), was a distinguished exemplar of Marburg success: an author (with books on American politics, world monetary problems, and international peace), an art collector, a proponent of city parks, a benefactor of Johns Hopkins University, minister to Belgium in 1912 during the Taft administration, and, though a Republican, an ardent supporter of Wilson's League of Nations. He was remembered as a quiet, slender, and elegant gentleman, and his mansion, at 14 West Mount Vernon Place in Baltimore, stood for many years as a reminder of his wealth and prestige.

Theodore's son, and Bill's father, Francis Grainger Marburg (November 25, 1900–May 10, 1988), after a distinguished education at St. Paul's Preparatory School, and then Princeton and Oxford, achieved success as an investment banker. Grainger, as he preferred to be called, worked first in the firm of Marburg and Price in Baltimore and, at the end of his career, as a member of the oldest investment bank in the United States, Alexander Brown and Sons, founded in Baltimore in 1800. Grainger married Mary Robbins Hocking, a local beauty, in 1922.[2] The Hockings trace their American lineage to William Hocking, a Cornish mining engineer who migrated to West Virginia sometime before the Civil War. Family members are unsure about the birthplace of Mary's father, George Hemming Hocking—it may have been Cornwall, or he may have been born after his parents arrived in the United States—but he seems to have been born in 1855.[3] He is remembered as a "country doctor" who made house calls in a horse and buggy (although he bought one of the first automobiles sold in the county) and often received payment with chickens, eggs, canned goods, and other forms of barter. His grandchildren loved to visit his office,

Wedding picture of Bill's parents, Mary Robbins Hocking and Francis Grainger
Marburg, June 24, 1922. Courtesy of Mary Lynn Marburg Brett

which was in his home, to see the many specimens that were preserved
in bottles. Unlike their Marburg grandfather, who was perceived as cold,
austere, and humorless, this Hocking grandfather was much beloved for
his gentleness, his understated but wry sense of humor, and his love of
music. The first music Bill ever heard may very well have been the piano
renditions his grandfather played for family gatherings.

Although her father is described as a country doctor who served a rural clientele, Mary nevertheless moved in social circles that were sophisticated enough to make her eligible for courtship and marriage to a Marburg. She went to Miss Frances Hoffman's Finishing School and made her debut in 1917 at the Bachelor's Cotillion, an event that introduced the socially prominent young ladies of Baltimore to eligible young men of their social class. Warm and lively, Mary seems to have settled easily into the life of the wife of a Baltimore aristocrat, and along with the social conventions expected of her—including her support of the city's symphony and opera—delighted most of all in the opportunities for world travel, a penchant apparently inherited by her son Bill. Mary enjoyed her family and loved to share journeys with them by steamship to the British Isles and the European continent.[4]

Although Bill remembers very little about his earliest years in Riderwood, his childhood there was decidedly secure and materially comforting, a welcome insulation from the hard times that were then ravaging the United States. He enjoyed the constant care of nurses and nannies, including one particular English-born nanny who took special care of Bill and pampered him. He received an exceptional education at Calvert,[5] a premier progressive, private K–8 school in Baltimore that four generations of Marburgs had attended, and which they still financially support. Both innovative and experimental, Calvert had instituted as early as 1906

Bill and sisters (left to right: Mary Lynn, Fifi, Martha, Ann, and Bill). Courtesy of Mary Lynn Marburg Brett

a program of homeschooling that permitted people around the world to use its curriculum to educate students who otherwise could not afford a good education or who could not physically attend the Baltimore campus. Calvert encouraged its students also to confront troubling issues and to think and talk about them freely. Bill, for example, remembers that he and his fellow classmates in the fourth grade explored the pros and cons of world government, and Bill was asked to write a paper on euthanasia. While living in Riderwood, Bill began also to exhibit a receptivity to music and its performance, an inclination that was never encouraged at home. His sister Mimi, however, did take piano lessons, and one day little Billy, then about six years old, climbed up on the stool and picked out with one finger the tune that his sister was trying to master. Only a little while later, when he was about seven years old, Bill heard someone at a party playing an accordion version of "A-Tisket, A-Tasket," an old nursery rhyme that Ella Fitzgerald rearranged in 1938 with great commercial success. For several years thereafter, usually at Christmas time or before his birthdays, he began asking his father for an accordion. Dad eventually relented and, before Bill's thirteenth birthday, rented an instrument for thirty days, saying that he would not buy one until Bill showed complete seriousness in learning how to play it. After Bill learned some Stephen Foster tunes and performed them for his father, Grainger then bought Bill his own accordion. Bill played the instrument for several years, at home and at parties, before it became too cumbersome and he turned his interests toward the guitar.

The Riderwood experience ended abruptly in 1939 when the Marburgs moved to a palatial home in Lutherwood, another suburb north of Baltimore and about forty miles south of York, Pennsylvania. While attending the 1939 World's Fair in New York City, Grainger learned that his father Theodore had given him an extraordinary present for his thirty-ninth birthday: an estate! Bought at auction, this was a splendid mansion, complete with about one hundred acres of surrounding land, a variety of stables, and dairy and farm buildings, which remained Bill's home until he went off to college in 1949. The house, then called Hambleton Hall, had been built on the model of an English country estate that its original owner had seen and loved. The Marburgs renamed the estate Selsed, after a ridge on which the property lay.[6] Although the three-story stone house was impressive—with its fourteen-foot ceilings, ten fireplaces, and leaded-glass windows—what captivated Bill most was the rural setting that framed the mansion. The years spent growing up at Selsed, in fact, constituted a formative and turning point in his life.

Bill in a pensive mood, about five years old, on the steps of his first home in Riderwood, Maryland. Courtesy of Bill Clifton

While Selsed was not exactly the "little farm" that Bill described in one of his interviews,[7] it was a working estate—built around dairy products and thoroughbred horses—that required much individual hard labor. Bill loved the opportunity to be outdoors, and, while he worked at the various odd jobs that were necessary to the maintenance of the farm, he particularly enjoyed milking the cows. This was a twice-a-day task, at about three-thirty in the morning before school began, and again in the afternoon. Farm life was so appealing to Bill that he subscribed to two farm journals, *Southern Agriculturalist* and the *Farm Journal*, and he began contemplating a college degree in agriculture, possibly at Cornell University.

Selsed House: Bill's boyhood home in Lutherville, Maryland. Courtesy of Bill Clifton

Barn and other outbuildings at Selsed. Courtesy of Bill Clifton

Bill's willingness to work brought him into close and daily contact with the hired hands who lived on the estate. Grainger really had no interest in involving himself in the grubby details of farm work, and had no need to do so, having inherited a farm manager and staff to keep the place going. The workers were not tenant farmers, as Bill has sometimes described them, but instead dairy workers, horse groomers, and gardeners who received free housing and utilities and were paid a salary twice a month. He found that these folks were decent, down-to-earth people with simple but positive moral values, characteristics that he easily found—and more significantly, identified with—in the music they loved (reminiscent of a slogan earlier used by the Carter Family to advertise their shows: "This program is morally good"). While Bill learned about some country music from his sister Ann, who listened each Saturday night to the broadcasts of the Wheeling Jamboree on WWVA in Wheeling, West Virginia, his most important exposure, largely because the music seemed to mirror their lives and experiences, came from the working folk there at Selsed. Leonard Snelson, the estate's head gardener, lived with his family in a small house just around the corner from the Marburgs. Occasionally, Bill visited at the Snelson home or rode with Mr. Snelson and his two sons, Frank and Tommy, in their Model A Ford, and listened to the radio shows that they favored. Mr. Snelson was an ardent country music fan, and he insisted that his sons and Bill listen closely to what they were hearing. Saturday evenings were particularly enjoyable, because on those nights Bill and the Snelson family heard the broadcasts of the *Old Dominion Barn Dance*, carried at 7:30 and 9:30 P.M., from the Lyric Theater on WRVA in Richmond, Virginia. Hosted from 1946 to 1957 by Sunshine Sue (Mary Higdon Workman), probably the first woman in America to have gained such a responsibility, the *Old Dominion Barn Dance* was one of several country variety radio shows that emerged in the late forties and was an example of the music's postwar commercial surge.[8] During the early years when Bill was listening to the show, the *Old Dominion Barn Dance* featured the music of such legendary performers as Marshall Louis "Grandpa" Jones, Mac Wiseman, and Mother Maybelle and the Carter Sisters (Helen, June, and Anita). Quite an indoctrination for a future country music star!

The country music that Bill heard in the forties was not yet universally labeled "country." That description, which was basically a marketing decision designed to lend respectability to the medium, did not take solid root until the fifties. The term most popular in Bill's time was "hillbilly," a usage that reflected the music's presumed backcountry or working-class origins. Neither fans, musicians, nor merchandizers took much care to differentiate among the varying styles heard in the music. Consequently, performers as disparate as cowboy singer Gene Autry, mountain crooner Roy Acuff, swing fiddler Bob Wills, and pop country vocalist Eddy Arnold

Bill, in his early teen years, with a favorite dog. Courtesy of Bill Clifton

were routinely marketed as "hillbilly." The music, though, increasingly exhibited a growing sophistication in the way it was presented and commercially marketed. Radio stations everywhere, large and small, featured country entertainers, and the record industry, which had suffered from the scarcity of shellac and other war-time restrictions, emerged as a vigorous and ever-expanding entity at the end of the forties. Although generally identified with the rural South, the music had in fact built a national profile, largely through powerful radio stations like WRVA, WWVA, WSM in Nashville, and WLS in Chicago. American servicemen had also taken

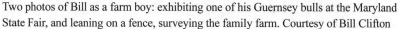

Two photos of Bill as a farm boy: exhibiting one of his Guernsey bulls at the Maryland State Fair, and leaning on a fence, surveying the family farm. Courtesy of Bill Clifton

the music around the world, and the Armed Forces Radio Network was introducing country sounds to the people of Europe and Japan.

In trying to understand why Bill fell in love with country music, it is hard to resist a quote made many years ago by the Oklahoma scholar Guy W. Logsdon,[9] a professional librarian, musician, and musicologist, at a music conference in Nashville. After hearing the theoretical observations of a number of commentators, mostly academicians, who pondered the popularity of country music, an exasperated Logsdon whispered to me, "Damn, it just *sounds* good." While we can never be certain why anyone embraces a certain style of music, and Bill Clifton himself would probably now be hard-pressed to explain his youthful conversion to country music, he nevertheless suggests that he found resonance in the belief that it came from "real people," decent, hardworking folk who inhabited a social context that appealed to his imagination. This was definitely not the kind of musical fare that one would have heard at the social soirees occasionally attended by the Marburgs. It also seems apparent that Bill's fascination and identification with down-to-earth folks was tinged with a strong admixture of romanticism that he has never abandoned, and which in fact has colored his perception of the music that he later made—the conviction that the music sprang from Appalachian roots.[10] The music Bill loved actually came from a wide array of origins, the mountain South for sure, but also from the vast rural recesses of the flatland South, extending from the Atlantic seaboard to the plains of Texas, and from the songbag fashioned by Tin Pan Alley (principally New York City writers, from the turn of the twentieth century) and the gospel hymnbook composers in the late nineteenth and early twentieth centuries. The hillbillies, whose music Bill had borrowed from their recordings, radio shows, songbooks, and public appearances, had drawn freely from minstrel, vaudeville, and any other entertainment sources that were available to them. The belief in the presumed "Appalachian origins" of country music, though, has been endlessly appealing to Americans, and hillbillies themselves—not unlike Bill—have been seduced by the notion that their music came not from the often sordid commercial interchange between rural and urban America but from a pristine, tradition-oriented, and semi-isolated way of life.

While Bill has persistently emphasized the supposed Appalachian beginnings of his and bluegrass music's origins, he has also had a lifelong fascination with the stories found in the music. The music he championed was disarmingly simple, in that it was easy to understand and perform, and it breathed with stories that could easily capture one's imagination. The music critic Nat Hentoff, long associated with New York's *The Village Voice*, has told a highly illustrative story of the great progressive jazz musician, Charlie Parker, who after playing hillbilly tunes repeatedly on the jukebox at Charlie's Tavern, a musicians' bar in midtown New York, told his incredulous musician friends, "Listen to the stories, man, listen to the stories."[11] Bill Clifton could certainly identify with this observation.

Sometime in late 1945, when he was fourteen years old, Bill made his first record purchases. On occasional trips into Baltimore, he visited the local record stores, which at that time were owned by the leading record corporations, such as Columbia, Decca, and Victor. After listening to records in a booth provided for customers at the Victor Record shop, he bought three Victor 78s by some appealing but quite dissimilar country artists:

Eddy Arnold ("I Walk Alone" and "Did You See My Daddy Over There");
Wiley and Zeke Morris ("Salty Dog Blues" and "Somebody Loves You,
Darling"); and the Carter Family ("Keep on the Sunny Side" and "When
the World's on Fire"). Bill's song choices, of course, were affected by what
was available in the record store, but the songs nevertheless tell us much
about the nature of country music at that time, and about the receptivity to
it felt by most fans. At that point in the music's history, one finds almost
no controversy among fans concerning the music's "authenticity." That
debate did not emerge until the late fifties in the wake of Elvis Presley's
style-bending experiments and the Nashville Establishment's efforts to
combat them. Eddy Arnold, known as the Tennessee Plowboy, was just
on the verge of becoming the top-selling country artist in America, and
though he sang in a smooth semi-crooning style, his plaintive songs were
popular with rural and working-class listeners. The melodious Hawaiian
steel guitar playing of Ivan "Little Roy" Wiggins, heard on most of Arnold's recordings through 1948, also contributed mightily to the Tennessee
Plowboy's success. The Morris Brothers, from Old Fort, North Carolina,
were unpretentious country boys who had been making music with various groups, most notably Mainer's Mountaineers, since the mid-thirties.
Performing with mandolin and guitar, their version of "The Salty Dog
Blues," recorded in 1938 and again in 1945, eventually became one of the
standards of the not-yet-emergent bluegrass genre. The legendary Carter
Family had been recording since 1927 and had completed their final session
only three years before Bill found copies of their records in the Baltimore
shop.[12] Bill had no way of knowing that all three of the Carters—A. P.,
Sarah, and Maybelle—were still alive, and that they would have an epochal
effect on his own career, or that A. P. would become virtually a father to
him. He did realize almost immediately, however, that among all the music
that he heard, the Carter sound and repertory were the most appealing to
him. They grounded his choice of songs and style of performance, and
became linchpins of his own career. And that feeling and allegiance have
never changed.

Country music became Bill's obsession. He had no serious girlfriends
until he was in college and seems to have had little interest in sports. He
listened to country music constantly, bought songbooks such as *Country
Song Roundup* and others produced by the M. M. Cole Publishing Company
in Chicago, attended concerts when they were locally available, and sang
country songs as frequently as he could.[13] He listened to his earliest record

purchases on the family's console radio in the main part of the house, and he remembers that his sisters were particularly fond of the Carter Family's "Keep on the Sunny Side." His sisters insist that Bill's father sometimes, surreptitiously, listened to the music as well. Bill's introduction to live professional country musicians came from concerts presented at scattered venues in and around Baltimore. For example, in the summer of 1948 he went to nearby Towson and saw a country variety show (usually described as a package show) that was promoted by the Washington, D.C., entrepreneur Connie B. Gay. Bill actually met and talked to the fiddler, Russell "Chubby" Wise, who had played with Bill Monroe in the mid-'40s when the bluegrass style was taking shape. Bill recalls that Chubby was "the first Blue Grass Boy I ever met."

Bill also attended concerts at one of Baltimore's most venerable venues, the Hippodrome Theatre (now the France-Merrick Performing Arts Center),[14] which since November 23, 1914, had served as the city's premiere site for movies and vaudeville performances. Seating three thousand people, the Hippodrome generally featured such nationally known urban entertainers as Bob Hope, Jack Benny, Benny Goodman, and Frank Sinatra, who is reputed to have made his first appearance there, in 1939, with the Tommy Dorsey Orchestra. Consequently, the appearance at the Hippodrome in the forties by people like Roy Acuff, Uncle Dave Macon, Red Foley, Sam and Kirk McGee, and Lew Childre signaled the growing acceptance and public visibility of country music among city dwellers. Bill does not remember the precise dates of the first country shows he saw, but he believes that they were in 1945 or 1946. He recalls reveling not only in the music he heard but also in the down-to-earth personalities of the performers, their warmth, and their willingness to meet and shake hands with their fans. A heavy rainstorm occurred prior to the first Hippodrome show, while Bill and one of his chums, Hamilton "Hap" Hackney, were standing at the back of the theater, hoping to catch a glimpse of the evening's entertainers. Trying to get out of the rain, they knocked on a back door, and when someone opened it, to their surprise they met Roy Acuff, who welcomed them warmly and introduced them to some of the other stars. They were actually fortunate enough to meet, and get the autograph of, the singer and five-string banjoist Uncle Dave Macon, the Dixie Dewdrop, who since 1926 had been a mainstay of the Grand Ole Opry. Bill enjoyed all of the country acts, but he was particularly drawn to the old-time rural performers. At a later Hippodrome show hosted by Red

Bill with childhood friend Hap Hackney. Courtesy of Hamilton "Hap" Hackney Jr.

Foley, he was swept away by the performance of Lew Childre, a veteran of country vaudeville who regaled the audience with his humor, buck and wing dancing, and old-time songs like "Riding on the Elevated Railway" and "Alabamy Bound."

Bill's teenage immersion in country music also brought him in contact with musicians much closer to home. Sometime in 1945 a friend named Billy Pierce told him about the country dances held in Fullerton, on the northeast outskirts of Baltimore, where Billy's dad and uncle often played. Pierce was only fourteen, but he was already adept at "Travis-style" guitar picking (a syncopated thumb and finger technique pioneered by the Kentucky musician, Merle Travis). Bill was learning how to play at this time, on a National guitar bought for eighteen dollars, complete with chord book, at a Baltimore music store. As the chord book advised, he played the guitar with a plectrum (flat pick) and did not know until several years later that one of his heroes, Maybelle Carter, used a thumb pick, along with a down thrust of her other fingers, to produce her distinctive sound. By the time this discovery was made, his own style was so strongly implanted that Bill continued to play Carter Family songs in his own fashion.

Although Bill learned a lot of songs, many of which he recorded on a Wilcox-Gay disk recorder, and witnessed the ways in which musicians interacted with each other, he seems to have played only infrequently at the Fullerton gatherings. These Fullerton sessions were held in a large, assembly-size room and were led by a dance caller named Bunny Shock. As he watched the dancers, Bill came to understand the social function of the music he loved, and he soon realized that the musicians and singers might stretch out a song like "New River Train" for multiple verses to accommodate the desire to extend the dancing. He did not then know who the Fullerton musicians were, but he has since speculated that they may have been Appalachian migrants who came from areas like Southwest Virginia, Eastern Kentucky, and southern West Virginia. They actually could have come from any number of other rural localities contiguous to Baltimore, or indeed could have lived in the area for many years. But as a thriving industrial city, Baltimore had certainly served as a magnet for rural migrants since the late thirties, and had experienced a particularly large influx during the war years, when workers thronged to the city's steel mills, shipyards, and aircraft industries. A similar movement into the Washington, D.C., area, less than an hour away, contributed to the making of a vast and interrelated urban region highly conducive to the emergence and popularity of transplanted rural music. Industrial and other blue-collar workers sought musical entertainment that provided escape from the drudgeries of their new existence while also bringing a touch of the old home. In Bill Clifton's musically formative days in Fullerton, the music was described simply as "country" or, more likely, "hillbilly." Ten or fifteen years later, the term "bluegrass" began to be widely used to describe one of the most tradition-based and exciting styles of rural string band music that began to flourish in the region.[15]

The country music that evolved in the Baltimore–Washington corridor in the late forties and mid-fifties was the product of a reciprocal relationship between rural transplants and urban fans. Rural musicians found places to play, as well as new fans who were socially different from their traditional followers back home. Musicians played not only in Baltimore and Washington area honky-tonks, generally frequented by working class-folk, but also in the house parties and country parks such as Watermelon Park in Virginia, New River Ranch in Maryland, and Sunset Park in Pennsylvania. New River Ranch and Sunset Park were only twenty miles apart; an ardent fan could visit both of them on a single weekend. At these locations, working folk rubbed shoulders with cultural bohemians or "folkies" who were just discovering grassroots music for the first time.[16]

The music also began to attract the attention of young people from urban middle-class homes, youngsters who in many cases were searching for something presumably more exciting or exotic than the music favored by their parents. No one has attempted a full-scale analysis of the reasons that motivated young urban people to embrace the bluegrass style, and the most prominent of these people—such as Pete Kuykendall and Richard Spottswood—have been hard-pressed to explain the fascination, saying simply that they found the music to be exciting. Another young musician, John Fahey, who grew up in Takoma Park, Maryland, and went on to become a master of finger-style acoustic guitar playing, was tongue-in-cheek in his recollections, but he may have come close to at least a partial explanation of this musical interest. Fahey argued that he and his youthful contemporaries were restless and bored, feeling that their striving parents were too busy to attend to their children's needs, but that they found not only excitement but community in the music played by Don Owens and other bluegrass disc jockeys. Fahey's own epiphany came one day when he heard Owens play, on WARL in Arlington, Bill Monroe's supercharged version of the old Jimmie Rodgers tune, "Blue Yodel #7." Once Fahey and his contemporaries made their individual discoveries, they began going to clubs and festivals in the Greater Washington or Baltimore region, listening to the numerous bluegrass bands that played there. In the mid-fifties these young fans contributed to the making of Washington/Baltimore as the bluegrass capital of America, and a few of them, growing up in places like Chevy Chase, Silver Spring, Bethesda, and Takoma Park—like Peter Kuykendall, Richard Spottswood, Mike Seeger, John Duffey, Tom Gray, Bill Emerson, and Eddie Stubbs—played prominent roles as musicians, producers, and popularizers of the genre. Only a few years earlier, and not too many miles away, Bill Clifton found himself in the vanguard of that movement, having embraced the music of his rural neighbors as early as

1945. By the end of the fifties, he was doing his part, as a musician and promoter, to popularize that music around the world.[17]

Fame as a professional bluegrass musician, however, had to wait. Bill first had to play a prescribed Marburg role. He had to embark on a course of formal education that would prepare him for the kind of social and economic leadership expected of a person from his particular class. And it was hoped that he would satisfy his father's dream that his son would pursue a conventional career in business. Consequently, Bill set out in September 1946 for Concord, New Hampshire, to attend St. Paul's preparatory school, where his father and grandfather had matriculated. While waiting for a northbound train at Penn Station in Baltimore, he met another young man, Hap Hackney, also headed for St. Paul's, who was destined to become one of Bill's best and most enduring friends. The Hackney and Marburg fathers had attended both St. Paul's and Princeton, and shared a common interest in horses and dairy stock. Hamilton Hackney was Chief Magistrate of the Juvenile Court of Baltimore and, at Cold Saturday Farm in Finksburg, Maryland, was a breeder of Charolais and Black Angus cattle, one of which was featured on the cover of *Time* magazine.[18] The school to which Bill and Hap were bound, founded in 1856 as an Episcopal boarding school, had become one of the most prestigious elite private schools in the United States and a prime bastion of WASP education. A later graduate and critic of the school argued that St. Paul's was a nursery of "adolescent elites" who were taught to be comfortable with privilege and to be unconscious of the role that hierarchy played in their lives.[19]

Bill seems to have adjusted well to the educational and social aspects of the school. His grades were adequate, and he was well liked. The five hundred or so students at St. Paul's were enrolled in four Forms, ninth through twelfth grades. Bill was elected as a prefect of the first Form, with duties consisting primarily of room inspections. In lieu of physical education, students were required to participate in intramural sports. Bill was assigned to the club to which his father had belonged, the Delphian Club, one of three athletic groups at St. Paul's; as a stocky young man, he starred on the club's football team. As an ice hockey player, however, a sport St. Paul's pioneered and at which it excelled, Bill was, in Hap Hackney's words, "an absolute failure."[20] Hackney recalled that Bill ran, rather than skated, on his skates. Although Bill sometimes played his accordion, music seems to have played only a negligible role in his life at St. Paul's, and except for Hap, he found no other country music fans at the school.

Country music, however, was no farther away than the radio, so he listened to various shows when time permitted and continued to buy records. He wrote at least one letter to Wiley and Zeke Morris, asking them to come to Baltimore to give a concert. They never responded.

Although he found lasting friendships and performed adequately as a student, Bill did not enjoy his experiences at St. Paul's. In fact, he did not graduate from the school. He was expelled.[21] Neither Bill nor Hap accepted the discipline required at St. Paul's, and Bill resisted particularly what he thought was the religious rigidity of the school. Mandatory attendance at chapel each morning soured him on formal religious observance, and he did not return to proper Episcopal practice until he was an older adult. His chief problems at St. Paul's, however, began with an incident involving a musical performance. Against the rules, Bill and another friend, Edward Palmer "Ed" Lincoln, went off campus one night to Manchester to hear a western-style band that was apparently somewhat similar to the Sons of the Pioneers. The concert ran late, and the boys missed the last-scheduled train back to the school. When they arrived at the train station, they found an open door into a small foyer but could not get into the station lobby itself. They settled down for the evening, but after Ed extinguished the overhead light, the police noticed the problem and arrested them. They spent the night in jail and then took the first morning train back to Concord, only to learn that Bill's dad and sister Fifi (Frances), returning from her school in Lennox, on the way home for Easter break, had stopped by the school for a visit! The trip back to Lutherville, after Bill's suspension, must have been acutely uncomfortable. During his one-term suspension, Bill was enrolled at Gilman's,[22] a former country day school for boys, and another distinguished private school in Baltimore. Although he knew no one and was generally unhappy at the new school, it was not a totally unproductive year, for Bill at least enjoyed the geography class, feeling that it opened up the world for him.

Ed Lincoln was not quite so lucky; he was expelled from St. Paul's and was not permitted to return. Ed apparently suffered little permanent damage from the expulsion, for he eventually became a distinguished professor of agricultural engineering at the University of Florida. He and Bill also remained good friends. During the summer vacation of 1947 they hatched an audacious plan to take an extended trip to Acapulco, Mexico.[23] The two sixteen-year-old boys came up with about $250 apiece and planned to hitchhike through the southern states and on through Mexico. But Bill's dad, remembering that his twenty-eight-year-old brother, Theodore Jr., had died in Mexico on February 24, 1922—apparently from a self-inflicted gunshot wound—was at first strongly resistant to the trip, particularly if it meant that his son might be wandering through the region on foot.[24] So Grainger eventually provided the boys a 1942 Ford automobile and his hesitant permission.

To Bill the trip was part vacation, part adventure, part geography lesson, part country music pilgrimage, and, ultimately, somewhat nightmarish. He and Ed first drove down through Eastern Kentucky and into the rugged coal country of Harlan County, the scene of much labor-related violence in the thirties. In the town of Harlan, a café owner exploited their curiosity by telling stories about the violent encounters (real and imagined) that had inspired the coinage of the term "Bloody Harlan," and then advised them to get out of town before nightfall. At another site in Eastern Kentucky, between Harlan and Jenkins, they encountered a much more beneficent scene, and one that was highly edifying to Bill's country music heart. He and Ed came upon a political parade that featured the recorded singing of Molly O'Day (born Laverne Williamson), one of Bill's favorite old-time country singers. He and Ed then drove down to Nashville, just in time to make the second show of the Saturday night *Grand Ole Opry* at the Ryman Auditorium.[25] This was Bill's first opportunity to visit the "Mother Church" of country music and to renew his homage to such heroes as Ernest Tubb, Roy Acuff, and Uncle Dave on their home turf. The pair then drove to Shreveport, Louisiana, for a visit to KWKH, a powerful fifty-thousand-watt station that featured a number of country music acts. The Shreveport trip came a few months before the inauguration of the *Louisiana Hayride*, a show that rivaled the *Grand Ole Opry* for several years, but Bill and Ed were able to see and hear some very important musicians, although they did not then realize that Kitty Wells (born Muriel Deason), whom they thought of as merely a "girl singer" (as women were promoted at the time), would one day be acclaimed as the "Queen of Country Music."

Bill and Ed were able to visit the early-morning KWKH broadcast of the Bailes Brothers, a powerful singing duo from West Virginia and one of the founding acts of the *Hayride*. Historically, there had been four Bailes Brothers (Kyle, Walter, Johnnie, and Homer), but at this particular time the Bailes Brothers consisted of the duet Johnnie and Homer, backed by their band, the West Virginia Home Folks.[26] Bill met a very friendly Homer Bailes and obtained some of the Brothers' songbooks. Leaving Shreveport, they crossed over into East Texas and headed west toward Dallas, hoping to see the great Canadian singer and guitarist Hank Snow, who they thought would be performing on the *Big D Jamboree* in that city. Hank, however, was on the road. Bill and Ed closed out their Texas adventure with a visit to one of Bill's pen pals, Wanda Kaufman, whom he had met through correspondence in *Southern Agriculturist*, and then with a jaunt to Fort Worth where they saw the famous Stockyards and enjoyed a juicy one-dollar steak.

It is almost staggering to think of the miles covered by these nervy teenagers on their journey to Acapulco. After seeing the sights of Fort Worth, they still had over thirteen hundred miles to cover before reaching the Mexican beach. But they journeyed on through Laredo and into Mexico City, where they saw a bullfight as well as their first glimpse of abject poverty. Bill particularly recalled the poignancy of seeing a little street urchin peddling candy from a wheel barrow after scurrying from his box home in a junk yard. Their generally successful trip floundered, however, on the Acapulco beach. They rented hammocks on the beach but woke up the first morning to find that their car had been broken into, and that most of their possessions, including Bill's Gretsch guitar, had been stolen. Luckily, the thieves had failed to look in the glove compartment, so Bill and Ed were able to salvage some travelers' checks. After a fruitless visit with the local police, who wanted some compensation before they continued their investigation, the boys began their long journey home. Somewhere along the road in Northern Mexico the steering column on their tired 1942 Ford froze, and when Bill applied the brakes, the car flipped over, and Ed was seriously cut by a broken coke bottle (fragments of which he carried in his body for the rest of his life). After eventually hitching a ride with a Texas-bound family, they made their way to Laredo, obtained medical aid for Ed, and then boarded a train for the ride back east. Fortunately, Bill had bought collision insurance on the trip into Mexico, and he was able to use the money for the train ride. He and Ed visited friends in New Orleans and Memphis, but made it back to Baltimore before the summer's end. And, amazingly, it should be recorded that Bill eventually got his Gretsch guitar back, and with only a minor scratch!

Bill had survived the Mexican caper, but his troubles continued when he returned to St. Paul's the following year. Rooming this time with Hap Hackney, he engaged in behavior that suggests that he wanted to be kicked out of the school. Drinking beer in their dormitory room was not unique, because other boys also indulged. Getting caught, however, proved to be their downfall. According to Hap, he and Bill inherited a "bootlegger," a local taxi driver who had been supplying beer for former student customers. During the winter months, Bill and Hap consumed the contents of a large number of bottles and then threw them out the window into the yard where they were concealed by the snow. When the snow melted, their sins were revealed. This time, Bill was permanently expelled from St. Paul's. He hoped to finish his high school education at a public school in Towson, Maryland, but his father quickly reminded him that "Marburgs don't go to public schools." He instead was enrolled in another unique and innovative private institution: the Adirondack-Florida School, a "migratory boarding school" that had two campuses, one near Onchiota, New York, where classes met during the spring and autumn, and the other at Coconut Grove, on Biscayne Bay in Florida, during the winter term.[27] Designed as a highly-selective college preparatory institution, and limited to only twenty-five students, the school had been founded in 1903 by Paul C. Ransom, who believed in the value of closeness to nature, a school where students could have one-to-one personal classroom instruction while enjoying the advantages of outdoor life the year round. A fellow classmate, Bill Ramsey, later jokingly recalled that Bill "only put up with formal education as a more or less necessary evil," and that his main interests were weightlifting and hillbilly music.[28] But Bill actually received an education at Adirondack-Florida that he cherished for the rest of his life, pleased that he had "teachers who were young enough to be funny, and old enough to be wise." He won the chance also to expand his musical horizons while enrolled there. The school required students to attend one religious service per week in a local church of their own choosing. Bill went to a variety of churches, including one from his own Episcopal denomination but found his most rewarding experience in a Pentecostal church, the Church of God. Bill still remembered those days with great affection many years later when he recorded what he described as his favorite album, *River of Memories* (Elf 103), a collection of vintage religious songs. Strangely, Bill does not remember any members of the Florida church speaking in tongues or otherwise practicing the precepts associated with Pentecostalism. But he fondly and admiringly recalls the basic and downhome qualities and musical zeal of the services. He clearly loved the singing and the music of the church string band and was warmly received in the fellowship of the worshippers. They called him "Brother Bill" and welcomed his guitar accompaniment.

Bill remembers their spirited singing of "I'll Fly Away" and probably some other Albert Brumley–composed songs. The Oklahoma-born Brumley, a frequent contributor to the music of the gospel quartets, was arguably the most beloved writer of religious songs in America.

Two other experiences concerning the church, however, forced Bill to reconsider his feelings about the spirituality he encountered there and about the economic basis of religion in general. When one of his Adirondack English teachers turned up his nose at the idea of Bill attending a Pentecostal service and asked him about the social makeup of the congregation, Bill told him that the congregants were basically working class. The teacher then asked if these people's loyalty to the church would endure if someone suddenly gave them a lot of money. In other words, would they seek a more prestigious church that reflected their improved economic standing? Although the question was clumsy, and fraught with snobbery, Bill seems to have received some insight about the link between money and religious preference. He remained loyal to his family's church but felt that allegiance to it was often the result of a class-based decision. His other experience made him question the spirituality of some of the people in the Pentecostal church, or at least made him aware of their materialism. One of the Church of God preachers shamed many members of the church while taking up collection, or so it seemed to Bill, by first asking for donations of one hundred dollars, and then for fifty dollars, before finally asking for any amount of money that they might have.

By the end of his high school years Bill had received an education of which few seventeen-year-old young men could boast, but only a small portion of it had been earned in the classroom. His self-confidence and resourcefulness, qualities promoted by his family's advantages, were bolstered by the experiences of his experimental youth. With country music consuming his every waking hour, Bill prepared for college, hoping to enroll at Cornell University and to pursue a degree in agriculture. His horizons at this time extended no further than the attainment of a degree, the return to the family farm in Maryland, and the fulfillment of the life of a country gentleman farmer.

2

FROM THE UNIVERSITY OF VIRGINIA
TO THE STARDAY YEARS, 1949-1963

While Bill's undistinguished academic experience in high
school may have jinxed his efforts to get into a prestigious eastern college,
he nevertheless succeeded in enrolling at the University of Virginia in
Charlottesville in 1949. This choice must have presented a pleasing "com-
promise" to his father. Sometimes described as "Mr. Jefferson's School," in
honor of the Virginia statesman and third president of the United States who
had conceived and designed its campus, the university is a beautiful and
eminent institution that prides itself in molding well-educated ladies and
gentlemen. It was, so many believed, the southernmost extension of the Ivy
League.[1] Grainger and Bill Marburg, however, arrived on campus too late
to secure a room in a dormitory. Instead, they found an apartment on Rugby
Road, which Bill shared with a young man named Todd Denigan. Rugby
Road was the center of fraternity and sorority life at the university and was
the site of a Georgian home once occupied by William Faulkner when he
was artist-in-residence at the university. Bill's dad deposited $1,000 in a
local bank to cover his son's first-year expenses and then headed back to
Lutherville. Tuition, however, was $675, and Bill immediately recognized
that this sum, added to the other expenses of books, living accommodations,
and social enjoyment would quickly decimate his father's contribution.
Grainger undoubtedly intended to provide more money as time went on,
but Bill probably wanted to achieve some kind of "independence" from his
father. That was a fantasy, ultimately unrealizable, an early instance of an

unresolvable pattern that negatively colored his relationship with his dad for the remainder of their lives. Bill managed to find a job as a cook and waiter at a local landmark called the Kitch-Inn, a diner that since 1922 had been located down at the Corner, a seven-block neighborhood of shops, bars, and eating establishments that lay right at the entrance to the main campus grounds. He also began driving a yellow cab two or three nights a week. Although Grainger was predictably outraged when he learned about his son's entry into the realm of blue-collar work, Bill was able to eat and otherwise support himself during his early years in Charlottesville.[2]

During his first year at the university, Bill took the required academic courses. But during his sophomore year, with the Korean War underway and military draft threatening, Bill chose a program that would be entertaining and easy, and that might ensure his making the dean's list (an honor roll of academic achievement that could inhibit or postpone induction into the army infantry). He decided to major in speech and drama. He found these courses to be interesting and, as he later maintained, immensely useful for the musical entertainment career that he ultimately chose. These academic studies certainly did not monopolize Bill's life, however, and his undergraduate years included a busy and well-rounded social life. He even went out for football but quickly abandoned that option after being roughed up in practice by a tough athlete from Beaver, Pennsylvania, named Joe Palumbo (a three-year varsity guard at UVA and an All-American in 1951).[3] Bill was definitely out of Palumbo's league! More successfully, Bill joined the Rho Chapter of Delta Phi Fraternity, founded in 1827 at Union College in Schenectady and generally known as St. Elmo's, the "oldest continuous" fraternity in the United States. The latter name derived from the fraternity's emblem, the cross of the Knights of Malta, of which St. Elmo was the patron saint.[4] Bill appreciated the camaraderie of the group, but claiming to have had few girlfriends during this period, he probably found the fraternity's most enjoyable social advantages to have been the free meals he received from waiting tables in the frat house. Of course, the exams from previous courses kept on file by the fraternity proved very serviceable, too. Bill admits that his A in geology may have been furthered by such support.

Feeling that a military draft might disrupt his college plans, Bill took the advice of his father's business partner, Bill Price, and joined the Naval Reserve Officers Training Corps (NROTC) in his first semester. "What a drag that turned out to be," Bill opined, when he realized that military training would consume the Saturday afternoons that he hoped to devote to music. As an alternative, Bill was told that he could transfer to the U.S. Marine Corps ROTC and instead fulfill his training obligations at Parris Island, South Carolina, in two six-week platoon leadership programs beginning in the summer of 1950. This decision freed his Saturdays but introduced him to what he remembers as "the hellish experience" of a summer marine boot camp in South Carolina. At his first camp he was told to bring only a small bag containing a change of underwear and shaving essentials. When he emerged from the train, carrying instead a guitar case with his Gretsch guitar, drill sergeant McNair, a grizzled and oft-wounded veteran of World War II, responded to this seeming impudence with a profanity-ridden tirade. Bill then proceeded to open the case to show that he had removed the strings and had stuffed the required essentials into the hole of his guitar. To make matters worse, Bill learned that Sergeant McNair, whom he uncharitably described as a Georgia Cracker, had a strong animus against college-educated recruits. But luckily, the sergeant turned out to be a country music fan. One day when Bill was strumming his guitar in the barracks, the sergeant asked him if he knew "The Soldier's Last Letter," an Ernest Tubb song about a mother's love for her son who had been killed in action. As the sergeant listened, with tears streaming from his eyes, Bill knew that he—and music—had converted a potential adversary into a friend.

The incident also reveals the powerful role that country music was already playing in Bill's life. While he did become involved in a variety of activities at UVA, music remained his passion, and he had added other instruments, such as the mandolin, banjo, and autoharp, to his performing repertory. He had also started looking for other musicians who shared his enthusiasm. Soon after enrolling at the university, he placed an ad in the school paper, the *Cavalier Daily*, asking to meet anyone who wanted to play and sing country music. He received five or six responses, but the most notable reply came from a student who already had considerable experience as a performing musician and ballad collector. This was Paul Clayton Worthington, better known as Paul Clayton, from New Bedford, Massachusetts (born on March 3, 1931), who, as a teenager, had already performed sea shanties, whaling ballads, and other traditional songs on the radio in his home state and was now working as an assistant to the noted University of Virginia folklorist Arthur Kyle Davis Jr. Davis's *Traditional Ballads of Virginia*, published in 1929, was one of the most re-

Bill (right) with Paul Clayton. Courtesy of Bill Clifton

spected collections of Southern-based folk music, and he was well into the
preparation of *More Traditional Ballads* when Clayton joined the venture.[5]
Clayton sang occasionally on WCHV and WINA in Charlottesville and
also conducted his own independent folksong collecting ventures in the
Appalachian South. He had rented a primitive log cabin at Brown's Cove,

near Crozet, in western Albemarle County, Virginia, where he hosted occasional picking and singing sessions. One picker who supposedly made
his way to the cabin a few years later was Bob Dylan, who shared songs
and melodies with Clayton and at one point was reputed to be his lover.
By the time Clayton died on March 30, 1967, a victim of suicide, he had
become a pillar of the folk revival in Greenwich Village, with an extensive assemblage of LPs on Folkways, Elektra, and other labels. His most
notable composition, "Gotta Travel On," became an oft-performed song
in both country music and the Folk Revival. Although Clayton did not win
the kind of lasting fame enjoyed by his friend Bob Dylan, he did achieve
a degree of posthumous recognition in 2013 in a popular movie about the
folk revival called *Inside Llewyn Davis*. Producers Ethan and Joel Coen
and actor Justin Timberlake found a photograph of Clayton wearing a
sweater and sporting a chin-strap beard and tried to approximate the look
in the character played by Timberlake.

In late 1949 and the early 1950s, though, Clayton had not yet achieved
national recognition as a folk singer. But he had a beautiful baritone voice
and was willing to experiment with the songs Bill loved. Although they
sang together at parties and jam sessions, particularly in the rooming house
where Paul lived, by 1950 they were also making separate appearances at
various public venues. For example, in that spring each played sets independently of each other at the Virginia Folk Festival, an event sponsored
by the noted North Carolina folklorist Bascom Lamar Lunsford and held
in the university gym. They were also making separate radio appearances
in Charlottesville, Bill on WINA and Paul on WCHV. Occasionally trying their luck as a vocal duet, they called themselves the Clifton Brothers
(Harvey and Bill). Clayton adopted the name Harvey from the invisible
rabbit featured in the Jimmy Stewart movie of the same name. Playing with
fellow students Dave Sadler (banjo) and Carl Boehm (bass), Bill and Paul
also ventured into the realm of bluegrass, a style that neither had earlier
attempted.

Johnny Clark, a non-student friend of Dave Sadler, occasionally brought
his five-string banjo to play and sing with them, and the group began
practicing hard with the anticipation of making public performances and
possibly landing a recording contract. In class and social background, they
were far different from Bill Monroe, Lester Flatt, Earl Scruggs, and other
founding fathers of bluegrass. In fact, they anticipated the diversity in
background that characterized many of the bluegrass bands that emerged

in the upper Seaboard South in the late fifties. Clayton's father was a salesman and executive for the Evans Case Company in North Attleboro, Massachusetts; Sadler was born in India as the son of an Esso geologist; and
Johnny Clark was the son of a show business entrepreneur who had moved
from New York to Warrenton, Virginia, in 1945, where he established a
ranch that specialized in Aberdeen-Angus cattle. Unlike the first generation
of bluegrass entertainers who had appeared in the wake of Bill Monroe's
experiments, none of these young musicians came from working-class
backgrounds, and only Bill Clifton was Southern born. Once Bill and his
friends felt reasonably confident about their ability to play together, they
made their way to a studio in the Speech and Drama Department, where
they recorded fourteen songs. Working before three microphones, Paul
played guitar and sang the lead vocals, while Bill played the mandolin and
did most of the harmony work. Clark played banjo on a few songs and
sang tenor harmony with Bill on a couple of numbers. They had chosen
a completely traditional repertoire—such hoary tunes as "Jesse James,"
"Old Ruben," "Bury Me Beneath the Willow," and "The Fox"—but they
also included at least a couple of Carter Family tunes like "East Virginia
Blues" and "Worried Man Blues." Bill sent the recordings to producer Bob
Harris at the Stinson label in New York, hoping that they would find their
way onto an LP, but they were not released.[6]

In the meantime, the audacious Bill had already embarked on his own
solo career. Before he moved to Charlottesville, he had scarcely played or
sung outside his bedroom, and almost never with anyone else, other than
the people he heard on recordings. Now, in the spring of 1950, after a few
short months of informal playing at jam sessions and dances in the city,
he was teaching guitar at the Don Warner Studio, which was next door
to radio station WINA in the same building. The station manager became
acquainted with Bill and soon asked him to do an early morning radio show.
Beginning on March 28, armed only with his guitar, and occasionally an
autoharp, Bill performed from 5:30 to 6:00 each morning. The young man
certainly could not be accused of lacking self-confidence. He had bought a
black Oscar Schmidt autoharp when he was seventeen but had never seen
Maybelle Carter play the instrument. Consequently, he laid the autoharp
on a table and strummed it, unlike the fashion favored by Maybelle, who
held it against her chest. He had somehow also managed to learn a few
chords on the mandolin and five-string banjo. Occasionally on the show,
Bill put the guitar aside, played a 78 rpm recording, and asked his listen-

Bill with banjo, WBAL (Baltimore). Courtesy of Bill Clifton

ers to guess who the performer was. One morning he selected a song that later played a profound role in his own emerging professional career: the Cope Brothers' version of "Mary Dear," an oft-recorded love song from the late nineteenth century about a soldier who returned wounded from war to find his sweetheart dead.[7] Commercially successful as one of his early recordings, Bill was still singing the song through the first decade of the twenty-first century.

The WINA gig lasted about a year, but in the meantime Bill branched out to other stations, such as WBLT in Bedford, Virginia, where he played three Saturday programs at 8 A.M., noon, and 6 P.M., and at WMBG in

Richmond, and WBMD in Baltimore. The Baltimore shows came during his summer break in 1950. His growing local prominence, especially on Baltimore radio, inspired his adoption of the moniker "Bill Clifton," used as a device to avoid embarrassment to his family. The name Clifton, selected from about ten different possibilities, seems to have been picked at random and had no relationship to anyone dead or alive.[8] Bill earned no money from these shows, but as a confirmed romanticist, he must have felt great satisfaction in pursuing, at least to a limited degree, the same kind of lifestyle fashioned by his hillbilly heroes. One finds supreme irony in the decisions made by this affluent son of an investment banker performing on an early morning radio show, asking the "friends and neighbors" for their cards and letters, calling himself either "the Yodeling Mountaineer" or "the Shenandoah Balladeer" (on WBLT) and hawking his picture-song book. He even advertised his shows in the national entertainment trade magazine *Billboard*.[9] He also learned new songs, honed his vocal and guitar skills, enhanced his public-speaking skills, and made new contacts in the hillbilly music field. For example, the widow of Roy Hall, a popular North Carolina hillbilly singer and leader of the Blue Ridge Entertainers, who had died in an automobile accident in 1943, contacted him, encouraged him, and sent him some songbooks.[10]

Bill, as we have seen, was in no way bashful about reaching out to entertainers he admired. Once, on a trip with his mother during one of her frequent excursions to New York City, he made an unsolicited visit to the office of the publisher and songwriter, Bob Miller, who had been one of the earliest independent writers in the hillbilly field.[11] Originally a jazz band leader in his hometown of Memphis, Tennessee, Miller had gone to New York in 1922 as an arranger for Irving Berlin, but by 1933 he had formed his own publishing company and had become a prolific writer of hillbilly songs—including "Twenty One Years," "Eleven Cent Cotton and Forty Cent Meat," and "Rocking Alone in an Old Rocking Chair." He cordially welcomed Bill and, after a lengthy chat, gave him a batch of song sheets and songbooks, and continued to send him such material until his death on August 26, 1955.

While in New York, Bill also visited with Harry West, an old-time musician and record and instrument collector who had moved with his wife Jeanie to the Big Apple from Statesville, North Carolina. It is no surprise that Bill found his visits to the home of Woody Guthrie much more memorable. He and Paul Clayton had often talked about the great Okie poet and singer, and they had frequently performed his songs, particularly those Woody had sung with Cisco Houston. In 1940 Guthrie had moved from California to New York City, where he became a catalyst for a burgeoning folk music revival.[12] So in the summer of 1950, when asked to accompany his mother on yet another New York City shopping holiday, Bill seized the chance to make an unannounced visit to Guthrie at his Coney Island home on Mermaid Avenue. To his great delight, Woody opened the door when Bill knocked, invited him in for a long friendly chat, gave him some songs, and encouraged further correspondence. Bill valued the letters he sometimes received from Guthrie, particularly a lengthy, single-spaced note written on "Happy Chanukah" paper on January 8, 1951, arguing that Bill should not have joined the marines while at UVA but instead should have enlisted in the merchant marines, as Guthrie had done during World War II.

Bill had sent Woody a photograph taken at WINA, and Woody replied with the observation that Bill looked like "a single man that sings a single song. Single now, but you won't be single long" (a play on a Carter Family song, "Worried Man Blues," that Woody had long been performing). Bill prepared his first songbook in 1951—a slender and modestly made folio called *Bill Clifton's Folio of Favorite Old Time Folk and Gospel Songs*. Featuring a cover photo of Bill standing and holding a guitar in front of a WBLT microphone in Bedford, Virginia, the book contained mostly traditional songs, except for the recent hit "Mocking Bird Hill" and a couple of songs Bill himself had written. He also pulled off a coup when he persuaded Woody to write the foreword; he wrote "You can't beat this book!" At times when the erratic Woody was out on some unexplained jaunt or otherwise unavailable, Bill met at least two future folk music greats in the Guthrie home. The first was Woody's three-year-old son Arlo, who had been set loose in his bohemian household wearing only a little shirt. The other was Elliott Charles Adnopoz (better known as Jack Elliott), who was then a math student at the University of Connecticut but was already on his way to becoming one of the greatest Woody Guthrie disciples, and only a few years away from his historic first visit to England.

The relationship Bill valued most highly also began in 1950, when he learned that A. P. Carter was still alive and living in Maces Spring, Virginia, only a four-hour drive from Charlottesville. Bill typically listened to the radio between classes, and one morning, while listening to WFLO in Farmville, Virginia, he learned that Carter was making a surprise appearance at 11:30 on Bill and Mary Reid's thirty-minute country show. Bill

Reid announced, "Folks, don't touch that dial. You won't believe who's in the studio today!" Carter sang "The Storms Are on the Ocean," a song the family had performed during their very first recording session in Bristol, Tennessee, in August 1927.

The following spring semester, Bill took a course on rural sociology that required a paper detailing the demography and economic statistics of a selected Virginia county. Bill chose to fulfill the assignment by writing about Scott County, the home of the Carter Family. One day he drove down to Maces Spring, and after a few inquiries he found A. P.'s son-in-law cutting the grass outside his house. A. P. was right inside—sitting on a couch listening to the radio. The glory days of the Carter Family had long passed, and A. P.'s marriage to Sara had disintegrated even earlier, but he had retained his passion for music and remained dedicated to the Family's heritage and history. He was pleased to encounter a young fan and was more than ready to share his memories and music with Bill. This first visit consumed at least three hours and completely solidified Bill's devotion to the Carter Family legacy. In the years that followed (before A. P.'s death on November 7, 1960), A. P. and Bill became intimate friends and musical colleagues. Bill visited him frequently at A. P.'s country store, slept in one of the double beds there, shared breakfast with him at his daughter Gladys's house each morning, drove A. P. to the bank, barber shop, or post office, took long walks with him, and sometimes sang with him on a radio station in nearby Kingsport, Tennessee. Occasionally, A. P. would take Bill on a long walk out into the country to take a drink from a local, favorite spring.

Despite his admiration for the country patriarch, Bill learned that the stories about A. P.'s eccentricities were indeed true. A. P. often slept in his clothes (and sometimes his shoes), and when singing with Bill, even on their radio appearances, he would sometimes quit in the middle of a song to go gaze out the window.[13] Apart from A. P.'s peculiarities, Bill found him to be a very proud man who was conscious of the Carter Family's contributions and of his own role in the making of American music. One night at a concert in Kingsport, Tennessee, Bill became acutely aware of A. P.'s pride and of the esteem other musicians had for him. He and Bill had gone to the Dobyns-Bennett High School auditorium to see a performance by the Chuck Wagon Gang[14]—a legendary group of Texas gospel singers whose names also happened to be Carter—and A. P. went to the musicians' entrance at the auditorium and asked for admittance. Insisting that "musicianers" always entered a performing arena in that way, he won immediate respect from the person who opened the door and from Wally Fowler, the singer and entrepreneur who had produced the show.

As A. P. was forty years older than Bill, their relationship was almost that of a father and son. Bill evidently relished the warmth and shared interest with his mentor that he had never enjoyed with his father. A. P. even tried to "fix Bill up" with a local girl, sixteen-year-old Peggy Hensley, hoping that marriage would tie him down to the community and force him to settle in Southwest Virginia. Although Bill and Peggy had a couple of dates, the relationship never blossomed romantically.

While Bill was forging these important personal associations, he was also working to extend his professional music career beyond the sphere of radio performances. The recordings made in 1952 with Paul Clayton, Dave Sadler, Carl Boehm, and Johnny Clark marked the genesis of the Dixie Mountain Boys, the title used for Bill's band at various times during his professional career. He used a varied assemblage of musicians during the fifties, and in fact later declared that he did not really have a permanent band after 1957 (although his recordings generally listed the Dixie Mountain Boys as his accompanists).

By 1953 Bill and Paul sang together only infrequently, but Bill had become more closely associated with other musicians, the most important being the young banjo player from Warrenton, Virginia, Johnny Clark. It is difficult to know exactly what Bill intended to do with this band, and even he may not have known at the time what direction he should take. The two words, "Dixie" and "mountain," suggest a Southern Appalachian emphasis, but whether the music was to be exclusively "old time" or whether it was to be a part of the current bluegrass movement is unclear. Bill later maintained that his intention had been to play and sing old-time music, probably in the vein of Mainer's Mountaineers, and that the Dixie Mountain Boys' identity as a bluegrass group was purely accidental. The direction taken by the band was shaped in large part by the banjo playing of Johnny Clark, a master of the three-finger Scruggs style. Despite Bill's protestations, the bluegrass identification became central to his identity and popularity.

It is now generally acknowledged that the bluegrass style began to take shape in the mid-forties in the music made by Bill Monroe and his band, the Blue Grass Boys (named in honor of Monroe's home state of Kentucky). The basic ingredients associated with the style—hard-driving rhythm, high lonesome vocal harmonies, a penchant for tradition-flavored songs, and the syncopated banjo playing of Earl Scruggs—set this music apart from other varieties of country string band styles. Until some undetermined date in the mid- or late fifties, this music was considered to be just another form of hillbilly music. But, gradually, fans, collectors, and publicists began to describe it as "bluegrass," an obvious recognition that something unique and appealing was taking shape in Monroe's band and among those who had been influenced by it.[15] Lester Flatt and Earl Scruggs, who had played with Monroe in the mid-forties, formed their own group, the Foggy Mountain Boys, and took the music to greater commercial heights and to audiences all over the United States. Scruggs-picking had attracted imitators all over the country, and the syncopated sound, if not the style, was even being adapted to other instruments, such as the mandolin, dobro steel guitar, and standard guitar. Johnny Clark had become one of Earl Scruggs's most passionate disciples.

John M. "Johnny" Clark was born on January 8, 1934, in Cincinnati, where his father worked as manager of the fifty-thousand-watt station WLW.[16] His mother, Elvira, had performed earlier with her sisters as a singer and dancer in a vaudeville act called the Giersdorf Sisters. In 1940 the family moved to New York, and the senior Clark became a producer and director of television soap operas. After 1945 the Clarks lived in Warrenton, Virginia, on a farm that Johnny's father had bought. They also invested in a gun shop that Johnny and his brother Jim later inherited; by 1960, it was reputed to be the largest gun dealership in Virginia. Soon after the move to Warrenton, Johnny set out to master Scruggs's syncopated three-finger banjo style. For a couple of years, he played with his own bluegrass band, the Green Mountain Boys, before joining Bill Clifton to form the original version of the Dixie Mountain Boys.

Johnny was a good-natured, rotund young man who brought to the band both a fine tenor singing skill and a dynamic, hard-driving banjo style. His banjo playing lent a distinctive stamp to the Dixie Mountain Boys and, according to Bill Clifton, defined how the band would be perceived and marketed. Bill insists that his music was essentially old-time country—that was certainly true of his repertory—but that Johnny Clark's banjo style gave it a flavor that permanently linked it to the bluegrass genre. However defined, the Dixie Mountain Boys found 1953 to be a tough year for a fledgling musical group. Although the band's personnel changed from time to time, the members making the first bluegrass recordings for Blue Ridge in 1954 included Bill, Johnny Clark, Curley Lambert (a veteran bluegrass

Bill and one version of the Dixie Mountain Boys, 1959 (Mike Seeger, Johnny Clark, John Duffey, Bill Clifton). Courtesy of Bill Clifton

mandolin player), Bill Wiltshire (fiddle), and Jack Cassidy (bass). Bill was then playing as often as his college classes and military requirements permitted, but musical engagements came few and far between. These included a couple of radio appearances in Richmond, a television show in Asheville, and shows at "The Barn" in Savannah (a large pavilion designed for weddings) and at WEAS in Decatur, Georgia. Bill also worked briefly as a DJ on WXGI in Richmond, on a show that lasted five and a half hours each day. The highlight of the year, though financially unproductive, was the band's short stint at WWVA on the *Wheeling Jamboree* in West Virginia. WWVA was a powerful station with signals that could be heard in Pennsylvania, Delaware, New Jersey, New York, New England, Ontario, Quebec, and Atlantic Canada. During the 1950s a thirty-minute block of the WWVA Jamboree was simulcast over the CBS radio network as part of the show *Saturday Night—Country Style*, which featured other barn dances such as the *Big D Jamboree* in Dallas and the *Old Dominion Barn Dance* in Richmond.

Sometime in early August 1953, Bill and the boys learned that one of the most popular WWVA *Jamboree* acts, the Davis Sisters (actually Betty Jack Davis and Mary Frances Penick, who performed under the name of "Skeeter" Davis), had been involved in an automobile accident on August 2 near Cincinnati, and that Betty Jack Davis had died. The Davis Sisters, whose harmonies were somewhat similar to those of the Everly Brothers, had recorded one super hit, "I Forgot More than You'll Ever Know." Sensing that a replacement for the duo might be needed on the Jamboree, Bill put his college career on hold, contacted the show's management, and secured a position for the Dixie Mountain Boys on both a morning show and the Saturday night barn dance. The boys moved into an upstairs flat in Moundsville (about eleven miles south of Wheeling, and once the site of the West Virginia state prison) and sometimes had to share their meager rations with a couple of other young musicians from the South, Buzz Busby (Bernarr Busbice) and Jack Clement, who were also trying to win spots on the popular country show. Required to wear appropriate stage clothes (which in the 1950s generally meant cowboy costumes), Bill bought string ties, Stetson hats, and matching trousers for the trio. In addition to their one-hour morning show—which included other musicians such as Lone Pine (Hal Breaux), Hardrock Gunter, and Dusty Owens—and Saturday evening performances, the Dixie Mountain Boys made occasional tours with other *Jamboree* entertainers. The most memorable of these came right after Labor Day and extended for three weeks from Wheeling up through New England and included performances in Grange Halls and drive-in movie theaters.[17]

The stint in Wheeling lasted for six months—from July to November—but aside from obtaining a panoramic insight into live-radio-performing life, the tour brought little acclaim or money. As the headliner of the act, Bill received eight dollars a day, while Johnny and Winnie earned six. Recognizing that decent-paying jobs would be few and far between November and the spring, Bill and the boys left Wheeling and went back south, hoping that other lucrative and secure jobs might materialize. Fiddler Winnie Sisk, whose problems with alcohol were becoming a hindrance to the group, went back home to Culpepper, Virginia, and Bill and Johnny drove down to Maces Spring to consider an option that A. P. Carter had negotiated with station WKIN in Kingsport, Tennessee. The station's initial offer of $125 a week, however, did not materialize. Johnny went back to the farm, and Bill returned to UVA to complete his college career, as well as the post-college military service required by the ROTC. At the end of the school year in 1953, Bill lacked seven hours to graduate, but with the aid of some correspondence courses, he received the bachelor of arts degree the following year.

Although Bill fulfilled his military obligations from the winter of 1954 to June 1956—he served as a communications officer in the U.S. Marine Corps and attained the permanent rank of first lieutenant—the complications of military service did not curtail his pursuit of a musical career. Quite the opposite: he continued to seek new ways of public exposure. In February 1954, in the midst of his Marine Corps training, he drove up from camp in North Carolina to Charlottesville to record again in the speech and drama studio at the university.[18] This time the recordings were made for the small label Blue Ridge[19] in North Wilkesboro, North Carolina, owned by Noah Adams and his daughter, Drusilla. Blue Ridge had been organized, in part, as a vehicle to allow song-writing Drusilla to get her compositions recorded by her friends, the Church Brothers. The label had enjoyed a modicum of success, particularly with recordings made by people like the Church Brothers, Wade Mainer, and Jim Eanes. Eanes's "Missing in Action" was particularly popular. It told the story of a soldier, once presumed dead, who returned home to find that his sweetheart had married someone else. Although the Adams's did not have enough capital to produce the records in very large quantities or to market them extensively, Bill decided that the recording was worth the effort. The Blue Ridge session included Johnny Clark, Curley Lambert, Bill Wiltshire, and Jack Cassidy. They recorded seven songs at their first session, the most memorable being "Flower Blooming in the Wildwood," a song probably learned from the Coon Creek Girls, and "Wake Up Susan," a tune featuring the twin fiddling of Carl Nelson and Carl Newman that seems often to have been played as a theme on radio shows. Bill was in fine voice, and his companions demonstrated that they had already evolved into a good, hard-driving bluegrass band. In early 1955 they recorded again for Blue Ridge, this time at a studio in Baltimore called Audio Services. Four of the five songs chosen were old-time numbers like "Railroading on the Great Divide" and "My Old Pal of Yesterday," while the fifth was a song that Bill wrote, "Take Back the Heart." Over the years he wrote more than one hundred songs, a body of material clearly influenced by his love for the Carter Family repertory and distinguished by his preference for old-fashioned metaphors and values. Like most bluegrass musicians, Bill could easily write and sing about cabin homes he had never inhabited, country churches he had never attended, and dead mothers to whom he had never been related. In this early recording session Bill again demonstrated his remarkable facility for finding outstanding musicians and utilizing them in his performances. One of the first of these was George Shuffler from Valdese, North Carolina, a guitarist and bass player who played the bass in an infectious walking pattern that, though well known in jazz, was then largely unfamiliar in bluegrass music. Several years later, while playing with the Stanley Brothers, Shuffler popularized a syncopated cross-picking style of guitar instrumentation (similar to the sound introduced by Jesse McReynolds on the mandolin) that ensured his eventual admission, in 2011, to the International Bluegrass Music Hall of Fame.[20]

Bill also made some important country music contacts during his military service. On leave one night at the annual banjo contest held in Warrenton, Virginia, Bill met a marine officer named James Owens, who happened to be a country music fan and, more important, was the brother of a disk jockey at WARL in Arlington, Virginia. Major Owens said to Bill, "I'd like for you to meet my brother; he's into country music, too." The brother, Don Owens, was indeed into country music! A highly influential radio announcer, he not only promoted bluegrass musicians in the Upper South, particularly in the Greater Washington area, but also contributed to the coining and popularization of the term "bluegrass" by using it frequently in his broadcasts. When the Blue Ridge recordings came out, Bill made them available to Owens, and through airplay on WARL, his versions of "Flower Blooming in the Wildwood" and "All the Good Times are Past and Gone" soon became favorites throughout the Washington, D.C., area. In the years that followed, Bill and Don Owens became friends and frequent collaborators in the booking of shows and the promotion of bluegrass and, in fact, became co-owners of the Blue Ridge label. Owens was consumed with bluegrass and spent many long and exhaustive hours touting it. He reputedly fell asleep at the wheel of his automobile at least three times after his late-night radio shows, the last of which, on April 21, 1963, resulted in a crash that took his life.[21]

The bulk of Bill's two-year military service occurred at Camp Lejeune, a 246-square-mile U.S. Marine Corps training facility in Jacksonville, North Carolina, and in Puerto Rico, where he did two summer stints. In addition to having a strong dose of personal charisma, he obviously must have impressed others with his natural leadership skills. As a result, Bill was named the commanding officer of a thirty-one-man communications platoon in the Second Marine Division. Despite his military responsibilities, Bill still had enough spare time to begin work on his famous songbook. He started writing down in longhand the lyrics of old songs, taken mostly from recordings, and eventually came up with more than enough to amass into a paperback book, which he called *150 Folk and Old Time Gospel Songs* (it actually contained 168). The cover showed an overall-clad farmer gazing at a distant cabin, presumably a representation of A. P. Carter engaging in a moment of rustic reverie. Augmented by illustrations drawn by his sister Ann, three thousand copies of the book were printed by his old friends from Blue Ridge Records, Noah and Drusilla Adams, but this run did not come close to measuring the breadth of the book's circulation, availability, and influence. Copies were passed around extensively or were duplicated by scores of people. Young musicians everywhere, who were just beginning to embrace the emerging bluegrass style, went to the book often to build or bolster their repertoires. Clifton's collection proved to be an essential resource during the folk revival at the end of the fifties, when musicians were looking for old songs.

One of the many musicians who discovered Bill's songbook was Michael "Mike" Seeger (younger half-brother of the famous Pete), who had already embarked on a campaign to document bluegrass and popularize it among his urban brethren. When he first found the book, Mike was living in Baltimore and was fulfilling his obligations as a conscientious objector by working as an orderly in a tuberculosis hospital. He and his friend Hazel Dickens, the great traditional singer from West Virginia, found time to sing in clubs and bluegrass jam sessions in Baltimore and were always on the lookout for old and singable songs. Bill's songbook became almost a Bible for the two young singers. Mike was also engaged as the producer of two recorded projects for Moe Asch, the owner of the Folkways label in New York City who had done much to trigger the folk revival with his seminal recordings of Woody Guthrie and Huddie "Leadbelly" Ledbetter.[22] One of Seeger's LPs was devoted to the documentation of Scruggs-style banjo playing, and the other was a collection of songs recorded by several bluegrass musicians, mostly from the Baltimore area. The latter recordings became the nucleus of *Mountain Music, Bluegrass Style*, one of the first albums ever devoted to bluegrass music, and a major force in introducing that genre to Northerners and others who were caught up in the folk music revival. Reading Bill's songbook, Mike learned from one of the picture captions that the illustrator, described as "Mrs. Carter Hoffman," was Bill Clifton's sister, Ann, and that she lived in Baltimore. Through her, he obtained Bill's address and soon began making trips to Lutherville, where he became a favorite of Bill's mother and sisters. Bill, on the other hand, eagerly welcomed the opportunity to work with Seeger, saying in a letter to him, "I would consider it a privilege to be of some assistance in your next recorded effort for the Folkways people." This was the beginning of a musical partnership and friendship that lasted until Mike Seeger's death on August 7, 2009.[23]

In the years that followed, Mike and Bill became very close friends. Bill loved Mike's sense of humor and his infectious laugh, and stood in awe of his remarkable musicianship. They played frequently in venues around the world. Mike also visited Selsed from time to time, and he, Bill, and Paul Clayton occasionally played in Baltimore for historical societies and society square dances sponsored by what Bill called his sisters' Social Register friends, and played on at least one cruise-boat excursion on the Chesapeake Bay. Bill insists that he won a new audience for old-time music through these cruises and soirees. Mike's versatility on a variety of instruments, most notably the autoharp, and his ability to sing a passable tenor, ensured his frequent participation on Bill's recordings and personal appearances. On a trip to the *Grand Ole Opry* Mike had discovered that Maybelle Carter, now playing on the show with her daughters, held the autoharp against her chest when she played. Armed with this inspiration, Mike became one of the premiere autoharp players in the world.

Largely in an act to bolster his economic needs, and to satisfy his father, who still clung to the vain dream that his son might become a businessman, Bill set out in November 1957 to earn a master's degree in business administration. With the assistance of the G.I. Bill, he enrolled at the Wharton School of Business in Philadelphia for one semester but completed his degree at the University of Virginia in June 1959, when his father chipped in for the remaining tuition costs. After graduation, Bill took a position with Chapman and Company, a media brokerage firm from Atlanta, finding buyers and sellers for radio and television time. Still living in Charlottesville, Bill began making weekly trips to New York City, staying in the Taft Hotel for five days and returning home each weekend (he may have found it appropriate to be staying in the hotel where country legend Jimmie Rodgers had died on May 26, 1933).

During this period, Bill also became associated with further media bro-kerage work through his association with Connie B. Gay, one of the most powerful personalities in country music.[24] Born in Lizard Lick, North Caro-lina, Gay was a Washington, D.C.–based music entrepreneur who had begun his career in radio in the 1940s with the Farm Security Administration's National Farm Hour. In 1946 he introduced a country music show, *Town and Country Time*, on WARL in Arlington, Virginia, which blanketed the Washington, D.C., area and contributed to the elevation of the music's im-age. From there he became an active promoter, booking *Grand Ole Opry* acts often in local arenas such as Constitution Hall. *Town and Country Time*, carried on both radio and television, provided a forum for the success of people like Jimmy Dean, Roy Clark, Patsy Cline, and George Hamilton IV. Gay was also one of the founders of the Country Music Association (CMA), created in 1958 to promote the legitimacy and commercial growth of the music. Bill Clifton's affiliation with Gay, buying and selling radio stations for the promoter, lasted only six months. But during a short stint in Nash-ville, Bill was offered the executive directorship of the fledgling CMA, a position he refused. Given Bill's magnetic personality, and his love for and commitment to the older sounds, he might have lent the CMA an approach more favorable to traditional country music than it ultimately assumed.

Although Bill's life had become less complicated when his service with the marines ended in 1956, his new business obligations could not have made his existence or his desire for music fulfillment any easier. Neverthe-less, he set out to resume and deepen his professional music career. He had become acquainted with the Stanley Brothers (Carter and Ralph)[25] a few years earlier, probably in Bristol, Virginia, during the Stanleys' lengthy stint on the noonday program, *Farm and Fun Time*, on WCYB. Carter Stanley[26] took a warm interest in Bill and his music and advised him to contact Walter "Dee" Kilpatrick about a possible contract with Mercury Records. Some of the Stanleys' most prized recordings had been on the Mercury label. Bill visited Kilpatrick in Nashville and played a demo copy of "Little White Washed Chimney." Kilpatrick liked the song, but he told Bill that he was leaving Mercury to take a position as general manager at the *Grand Ole Opry*. He advised Bill to get in touch with Don Pierce, his incoming replacement.[27] Pierce was destined to play a major role in Bill's recording endeavors and in his subsequent career in England and Japan. Born in Ballard, Washington, on October 10, 1915, Pierce (whose real name was Picht) became part owner in 1953, along with Jack Starnes and

Don Pierce of Starday Records. Courtesy of Nathan D. Gibson

Harold "Pappy" Daily, of the Texas-based Starday label.[28] In the face of the rock-and-roll invasion that followed the emergence of Elvis Presley in 1954, Starday became a powerful force in preserving traditional styles of country music through the signing of a retinue of outstanding musicians such as George Jones, Roger Miller, Red Sovine, and Frankie Miller.

Pierce moved to Nashville in 1957 and began an energetic and aggressive campaign to fill the niche left by country music's flirtation with rock and pop sounds. Starday, which severed its relationship with Mercury in 1958, promoted not only bluegrass bands but also recorded older acts, such as the Blue Sky Boys (Bill and Earl Bolick) and Sam and Kirk McGee, groups that had almost been forgotten. In recording Bill Clifton and the Dixie Mountain Boys, Starday was promoting both old-time music *and* the bluegrass style. When Bill went to Nashville in November 1956 for his first recording venture with Starday (at the RCA Studio), Bill's banjo player, Johnny Clark, was playing with Wilma Lee and Stoney Cooper's Clinch Mountain Clan and was unable to make the trip. Carter Stanley, though, again came to the rescue and recommended that Bill should take his brother, Ralph, with him as his five-string banjo player. Ralph Stanley played on the four songs that were recorded at that session but was not asked to sing because his distinctive, backcountry tenor would give the records a decided Stanley Brothers flavor. Only thirty years old, Stanley nevertheless already had the vocal timbre of an ancient mountain man. Bill, understandably, wanted his own sound. The Dixie Mountain Boys otherwise included the same personnel that had made the Blue Ridge recordings: Curley Lambert, George Shuffler, and Bill Wiltshire. An additional performer, fiddler Sonny Mead, provided the twin fiddling (along with Wiltshire) that Bill loved, and which helped to give his recordings their exciting sound. Bill was not the first bluegrass musician to feature twin fiddling—Bill Monroe and Mac Wiseman hold that distinction—but he used it in his most important Starday sessions and contributed some of the most vital and memorable sounds heard in bluegrass music during those years. The first two songs released from this session, "Gathering Flowers from the Hillside" and "Take Back the Heart" (Starday 290), incidentally, proved to be the first songs to appear in Starday's bluegrass catalog.

Bill's second recording venture for Pierce, in April 1957, was made under the auspices of the Mercury label. Held also at the RCA Studio in Nashville, the session was a landmark event. It included songs like "Little White Washed Chimney" (recorded for the second time) and "Mary Dear" that not only became widely popular in the bluegrass realm but also remained central and beloved ingredients of Bill's repertory for the rest of his career. Johnny Clark was back as a Dixie Mountain Boy, and, at his urging, was joined by some of Nashville's greatest musicians, acoustic bass player Roy M. "Junior" Huskey, who appeared on scores of recordings made in the city, and fiddlers Gordon Terry and Thomas Lee "Tommy" Jackson, all of whom were among the first active "sessions" musicians in what was fast becoming known as "Music City, USA."[29] Born in Decatur, Alabama, Terry was a veteran bluegrass musician who had played with Bill Monroe and had appeared on numerous recordings by other country performers. Jackson, from Birmingham, Alabama, was a remarkably versatile musician who was comfortable in any style, ranging from western swing to honky-tonk and bluegrass. He had been appearing on recording sessions since the late forties in Cincinnati and Nashville. Jackson almost singlehandedly kept the fiddle alive in country music in the years immediately following Elvis's emergence, partly by appearances on square dance recordings during a short-lived craze for that style of dancing during the fifties, and then through his work on Ray Price's popular shuffle-beat Columbia recordings later in that decade.

Bill's recording career extended for many decades after these initial efforts, but his tenure with Starday/Mercury, from 1956 to 1963, saw him at the height of his musical powers. His singing was strong and mellow, marked by faultless diction and articulation. His guitar playing was also exceptional. Most guitar players at that time followed the pattern set by guitarists in Bill Monroe's band, adhering solely to rhythm patterns and occasional bass runs. Several of the pioneer bluegrass guitar pickers, such as Clyde Moody, Lester Flatt, and Carter Stanley, played with thumb picks, a practice that inhibited facile single-string notation. Except for Don Reno, Bill Clifton was virtually the only guitarist in the bluegrass realm who played lead passages during a song. While some people described him as a "citybilly," an urban person who was trying to borrow or emulate the music of rural culture, one never had the sense that he was parodying or singing "down" to the music. Bill's treatment of a song was entirely appreciative and sincere. While he did not deal with all of the variety of songs in the country songbag—one finds no honky-tonk or cheating songs, for example—the songs he did choose were integral to the music's traditions and self-definition. They were generally older songs that breathed with nostalgia and reverence for old-time rural scenes, values, and customs.

Until 1961 Bill's work for Starday consisted exclusively of singles issued on 78 and 45 rpm recordings. His first LPs, *Mountain Folk Songs* and *The Bluegrass Sound of Bill Clifton*, issued in 1961, included only previously recorded singles. His music was also circulated, here and abroad, on Starday anthologies, described by *Billboard* columnist Bill Sachs as "Starday's packaged goods."[30] With names like *Banjo in the Hills* and *Preachin' Prayin' Singin'* (an all-gospel compilation), these collections were brightly colored, even garish affairs that caught the viewer's attention, while including brief, but not always accurate, liner notes, frequently written by Don Pierce. Pierce was an indefatigable merchandiser and publicist who often sent out packets of recordings to radio stations around the country. Bill's widely circulated records introduced many old songs to the record-buying public and meshed nicely with the desire for such music that emerged during the early years of the folk music revival.[31] Although the Kingston Trio's 1958 recording of "Tom Dooley" (their reworking of an old North Carolina murder ballad) set off an unprecedented enthusiasm for traditional or tradition-based songs, it should be noted that country and bluegrass musicians had in fact been preserving and reviving old songs well before the practice occurred in the folk revival. As early as 1947, for example, Merle Travis had released a very influential album of 78s for Capitol called *Folk Songs from the Hills* which, in addition to his own classic compositions, "Sixteen Tons" and "Dark as a Dungeon," had included several traditional songs such as "John Henry," "I Am a Pilgrim," and "Nine Pound Hammer." The Louvin Brothers' *Tragic Songs of Life* (Capitol, 1956), the Everly Brothers' *Songs Our Daddy Taught Us* (Cadence, 1958), along with the plethora of old songs heard in the recordings of people like Mac Wiseman, Flatt and Scruggs, the Stanley Brothers, Wilma Lee and Stoney Cooper, Hylo Brown, and Bill Clifton, indicate a strong and widespread hunger for old songs. Bill, as we have seen, thought of himself as a song carrier, a person who was interested in the preservation and renewed popularization of old songs that had been forgotten or ignored. He was not a folklorist, however. While he knew and acknowledged where he learned such songs as "Mary Dear" (from a Charlie Poole recording), "Little White Washed Chimney" (from Paul Clayton, who in turn had heard Slim McAuliffe sing it), and "Blue Ridge Mountain Blues" (from the singing of Wade Mainer), he did not bother to determine their original provenance. Singers nevertheless profited from Bill's rediscovery of such material—that is why they seized upon his famous songbook—and folklorists were provided with tools for the examination of old songs and their relationship to popular culture.

On September 3, 1960, at the Church of the Redeemer in Baltimore, Bill added a new dimension to his already multifaceted life. He married Sarah Lee Streett Ransom, born on January 20, 1932, whom he had known since their school days at Calvert in Baltimore. Their parents had known each other for even longer. Tad Marburg, Sarah's oldest son, described his maternal grandparents, Lettice Lee Coulling and William Busteed Streett, as "old southern aristocracy," people with less money than the Marburgs but with more prestigious lineage.[32] Sarah Lee had been widowed in 1958 when her husband, Charles Loren Ransom, was killed in an automobile accident. She was left with three small children—Charles Perry Randolph (Tad), David Streett Southern, and Katherine Lee Duval—whom Bill adopted and embraced as his own. He insisted that they keep their own last name, as well as that of Marburg. Bill and his new family moved into a big rambling farmhouse in Warrenton, Virginia, that was owned by Sarah Lee's family. They lived there from September 1960 to June 1961, and the house became a popular rendezvous for musicians and music industry people. For example, Dixie Deen, the British country music journalist and later wife of superstar Tom T. Hall, stayed with the Marburgs shortly after her arrival in the United States in 1961.[33] It was through Bill that she met and became a confidant and companion of Maybelle Carter. Mike Seeger and his wife Marjorie (Marj) also stayed with Bill and Sarah Lee for a few months during the early years of the Seegers' marriage (described by Mike as his "homeless" period). In the meantime, Bill and Sarah Lee got busy making their own family, ultimately bringing four more little Marburgs into the world—Sarah Lee Chandler, Jennifer Lee Cameron, William Francis Grainger, and John Rush Taylor.

By the time their Warrenton residence ended, Bill's six months with Connie B. Gay had dissolved, and he had taken a new position with a stock brokerage firm called Abbott, Proctor, and Paine (the forerunner of Paine Webber) and had moved with his family back to Charlottesville. They rented an antebellum home called Glen Echo at nearby Proffit. Although Bill likes to say that the house had been built by Thomas Jefferson for his slave mistress, Sally Hemmings, he may have succumbed to local and unsubstantiated lore, because no published source provides corroboration. Glen Echo, nevertheless, was an elaborate structure with its own unique charm, replete with eight bathrooms and many bedrooms, and was surrounded by thirty-five acres of woodland, meadows, and a pond. Many of Bill's musician friends, such as the Stanley Brothers and the New Lost City Ramblers (Mike Seeger, John Cohen, and Tracy Schwarz), appreciated the pond as a popular site for hunting and fishing. The Stanleys may have felt a bit too much at home at Glen Echo, however, because once, in the wee hours of the morning, they stopped by the house, hoping to find lodging for the night. With regret, Bill told them that, due to the presence of several of his visiting relatives, no room was available for them.

Bill with Mike and Marj Seeger. Courtesy of Bill Clifton

Regardless of how his employer may have defined Bill's relationship to the firm, he clearly never considered Abbott, Proctor, and Paine to be his only preoccupation. Music remained his first love, and he refused to allow business to marginalize his music career. The year 1961 proved to be, probably, his most productive year in the music business. Fittingly, Bill produced his first LP of newly recorded material as a tribute to the Carter Family. He had been accumulating an enormous cache of Carter songs since 1945 and had already fashioned a close relationship with A. P. and most of his family, including Sara and Maybelle, the two women from the original trio. After Don Pierce asked him to record an album of Carter Family songs, Bill eagerly set out to accomplish the task, eventually producing twelve songs, recorded in two long sessions extending over two days in Nashville at the Starday Record- ing Studios (March 1961) and in Washington, D.C., at Capitol Transcription Service (March 13, 1961). Regrettably, A. P. did not live long enough to see or hear the finished product. He passed away in February 1960. As he lay in an oxygen tent in the Holston Valley Community Hospital in Kingsport, Tennessee, Bill told him about the project but felt that A. P. never gained enough consciousness to comprehend the message.[34]

For the *Carter Family Memorial Album*, Bill wisely made no attempt to copy the Carters but instead performed the songs in bluegrass style, just as Lester Flatt and Earl Scruggs and the Foggy Mountain Boys did in their Carter Family tribute, *Songs of the Famous Carter Family* (Columbia), also recorded in 1961. Bluegrass, after all, had become the most important reposi- tory of Carter Family songs. Mike Seeger, who was actually skeptical of the decision to do the tribute in bluegrass style, provided autoharp accompani- ment, but not in the chorded style originally fashioned by Sara Carter. He instead played with the same melodious, individually noted style used by Maybelle when, in 1943, she organized an act with her daughters, Helen, June, and Anita. Mike also sang tenor on some of the songs, such as the affecting "Are You Lonesome Tonight?" "You Give Me Your Love and I'll Give You Mine," and "'Mid the Green Fields of Virginia." Don Pierce wrote the liner notes, providing basic biographical information about the Cart- ers, but went way off the mark when he said that "Bill was raised with the Carter Family in the Blue Ridge Mountains of Virginia" (a fantasy that Bill probably wished had been true). The album became well known among folk aficionados and old-time country music fans in both the United States and England, providing young singers with a useful repertoire of Carter Family songs and supplying a greater appreciation of the family's role in preserving old songs and introducing them to a wider public. The album seems to have been well received among most listeners and critics, but a few purists were offended by Bill Clifton's singing style or by the collection's departure from the Carter Family sound. Writing in the small but influential folkie magazine, *The Little Sandy Review*—published in Minnesota but widely circulated in the folk community—the acerbic critics Jon Pankake and Paul Nelson noted that Bill "had meant well," but that his singing was "blandness at its most irritating," and his accompanying instrumentation was "noisy and fulsome." Their final assessment was questionable, arguing that "the record will hold a position of tentative value on the market" until it was supplanted by "more knowledgeable revivalists of the Carter Family's songs and styles."[35]

In defense of Bill Clifton, it should be noted that no one anywhere was more knowledgeable about the Carter Family than he, and his singing style, appropriately, was his own. Vocally, he did not try to sound like the Carters or any other hillbillies. The country music authority and discographer, Richard Spottswood, praised Bill for singing with his own voice and for refusing to affect a hillbilly accent. Bill's music identity, however, admittedly had always been somewhat hazy, in that he teetered between folkiness and country, and an unidentified writer on the internet in fact once argued that Bill "was a folksinger who thought he was country."[36]

Although Bill frequently recorded old songs and sometimes used the word "folk" to describe them, he seems to have made little attempt to align himself with the urban folk-revival world that flourished after 1958 in the wake of the Kingston Trio's emergence. Bill's songbook, however, was apparently well known among northern bluegrass musicians, and Israel "Izzy" Young, the proprietor of the famous Greenwich Village bookstore and music emporium, The Folklore Center, sold copies of the book. But on the whole, the urban folk world seems to have made little attempt to embrace Bill's music, perhaps thinking of him as just another bluegrass singer. While his recording of "The Springhill Disaster," on November 5, 1958, was the kind of song becoming popular in folk circles, it was also reminiscent of the hillbilly event ballads of the 1920s, topical songs written by people like Carson Robison and Blind Andy Jenkins that capitalized on the news of the day. The disaster occurred in Nova Scotia on October 23, 1958, killing seventy-four miners and trapping one hundred who were eventually rescued. Bill's interest was piqued when he saw a poem written by an African Canadian, Maurice Ruddick, a survivor of the disaster. Ruddick had supposedly told his rescuers, "Give me a drink of water and I'll sing you a song." After a phone call to Ruddick obtaining permission to write about the event, Bill enlisted the aid of Sonny Pembroke and his old friend Paul Clayton, and fashioned a song that he recorded in Nashville at the RCA Victor Studio just two days after the event. He later included it on the LP *The Bluegrass Sound of Bill Clifton* (Starday SLP 159).[37] The song experienced considerable radio play in Halifax but had little success elsewhere; it was actually upstaged by another ballad about the event, a song written by Peggy Seeger and Ewan MacColl. Peggy was the American-born sister of Pete and Mike Seeger and, along with her husband MacColl, was well known for her protest songs and music of social commentary.

By 1961 bluegrass music had become well entrenched in American popular culture and had witnessed the proliferation of groups that had followed, more or less, in the musical footsteps of Bill Monroe, Flatt and Scruggs, and other pioneers. Bluegrass, though, had already begun to subdivide into traditional and progressive camps, with the Country Gentlemen, a band of young musicians from the Washington, D.C., area, leading the march toward stylistic innovation. Bluegrass musicians of all kinds, however, had to struggle to put food on the table and, since the emergence of rock and roll after 1954, had increasingly found many traditional venues of exposure closed to them. By the end of the sixties, though, bluegrass musicians had built a thriving subculture with its own journals, record labels, radio stations, and performing arenas. The most important of these, the festival, began to be held at sites all over the nation. Bill Clifton played a vital role in the popularization and acceptance of the festival alternative, and, in so doing, did much to energize a musical genre that had been languishing and was often hobbled by personal feuds.

Festivals, of course, had long been fixtures in American music, and the Newport Jazz Festival, held since 1954, was well known to country and bluegrass musicians. The bluegrass festivals also had precedents in the music heard at parks on weekends and in the religious camp meetings of the nineteenth century. Bluegrass festivals have in fact often been compared to the camp meetings. Held outdoors in rustic settings, mostly in the South, these gatherings were religious revivals where Protestant Christians of divergent backgrounds and opinions worshiped and sang in common fellowship. Similarly, the bluegrass festivals attracted fans from all walks of life—blue-collar workers, urban professionals, liberals, and conservatives—and featured both veteran and up-and-coming bands, while providing opportunities among fans for impromptu jam sessions. For many years, country and bluegrass musicians had played in parks, such as Roy Acuff's Dunbar Cave in Tennessee, Watermelon Park in Virginia, New River Ranch in Rising Sun, Maryland, and Sunset Park in West Grove, Pennsylvania, but these affairs had usually been confined to only a small number of acts. No one as yet had been bold enough to build a festival solely around bluegrass. Bluegrass bands that played in such venues, thus far, had been part of a mix that included country musicians of varying stylistic stripes. In 1961 Bill Clifton seized the opportunity to open up the parks to wider bluegrass exposure.

That year, Bill became the manager of Oak Leaf Park, near Luray, Virginia, about seventy-five miles west of Washington. Along with Marian Lewis, who owned a string of radio stations in the Shenandoah Valley, Bill began scheduling country music concerts at the venue, typically alternating each week between old-time and bluegrass acts and modern performers like Faron Young and Hank Snow. On May 28 the Stanley Brothers began the season that was to run through September 17. During that period Bill booked most of the active bluegrass bands then in existence. The keystone of the season came on July 4, when Bill and Marian Lewis presented a program of bluegrass music that was designed not only to bring top-flight entertainers to Luray, but also to reunite certain musicians who had played with Bill Monroe. Over the years, Bill had built a cordial relationship with Monroe, a towering musician who was not known for his approachability and who harbored resentments against those he believed had ignored or underplayed his accomplishments and importance. So in addition to Bill Monroe, Bill had successfully invited such seminal musicians as Mac Wiseman, the Stanley Brothers, the Country Gentlemen, and Jim and Jesse McReynolds, all of whom recognized Monroe's pioneering role and were eager to play with him.

This historic, one-day bluegrass festival was not the first one ever held, although it was long described in this fashion. Some bluegrass websites still applaud Bill Clifton as a pioneer and insist that if one enjoys going to festivals, then "thank Bill Clifton." Don Owens, though, had organized a similar festival, billed as "Bluegrass Day," at Watermelon Park in Berryville, Virginia, on August 14, 1960. Bill Monroe and several other bluegrass luminaries had also been present at this affair. Bill Clifton's contributions, however, should not be undervalued. His Luray festival was an important and widely heralded event that was attended by fans from all over the country and even from Japan (Tatsuo Arita, for example, who had long been encouraging young Japanese musicians to take up the bluegrass style, came down from New York with country record merchandizer David Freeman).

Bill had advertised the show on the Mount Jackson, Virginia, radio station, had circulated about one thousand flyers, and had managed to get Israel Young, proprietor of the Folklore Center in New York City, to promote the show among the folkies in that region. The festival had a respectable attendance of twenty-two hundred, although the advertising costs enabled Bill to clear only fifty dollars. Nevertheless, the crowd included several high-profile people in the folk and bluegrass communities, including Mike Seeger and several of his northern friends, such as Ralph Rinzler (who soon became Bill Monroe's manager), as well as David Freeman, the owner of County Sales and County Records (then located in New York City), who eventually produced some of Bill Clifton's most important albums.

While most people agreed that the music heard at Luray was superb, and that it was thrilling not only to see several of Monroe's former musicians playing with him again on stage and actually speaking to each other, the show was nevertheless plagued by controversy. If Bill Clifton's intent had been to build bridges or mend broken relationships, he was not entirely successful. For one thing, more than one commentator has argued that Bill may have erred in making some spiked wine punch available backstage, and that an inebriated Carter Stanley, who was fatally fond of the bottle, consequently waxed too frankly on stage. After Monroe commented about Lester Flatt and Earl Scruggs's conspicuous absence from the festival, Stanley sarcastically remarked, "We missed 'em a heck of a lot, ain't we?" Bill Monroe's long estrangement from Flatt and Scruggs, who had helped him create the bluegrass style, was well known, as was Carter Stanley's contempt for the duo. Not so well known, or at least ignored, was the fact that the remarks were being taped! Stanley's comments and Monroe's tacit agreement with them may have become known to Louise Scruggs, Earl's wife and manager (who nevertheless later denied that she was aware of the incident). Although several fans apparently taped the show, Bill Monroe became convinced that Mike Seeger and/or Ralph Rinzler, who were well known for their habits of taping country music performances, were responsible for news of the incident becoming widely circulated.

Bill Clifton, of course, while embarrassed by the episode, was nevertheless pleased by his success in bringing musicians together and making their artistry available to larger audiences. The practice of reuniting Bill Monroe with his former musicians became a standard fixture of bluegrass festivals. The Luray Festival was also a one-day anticipation, or microcosm, of the approach taken by other festivals after 1965, when Carlton Haney, an active country music promoter from North Carolina, inaugurated his multi-day, multi-group festival at Cantrell's Horse Farm in Fincastle,

Virginia, in September of that year. Haney had been present at Luray but had not participated in the event in any fashion. According to bluegrass historian Neil Rosenberg, Haney had originally disagreed with Clifton's idea, feeling that "there was no reason to have more than one bluegrass band" at a show. The notoriety of the Luray Festival also raised Bill Clifton's profile and made his name more widely known in bluegrass and in the folk revival community. Luray, in fact, may have contributed directly to his presence at the prestigious Newport Folk Festival in 1963.[38]

George Wein, the founder of the Newport Jazz Festival, organized a folk counterpart in 1959 that, incidentally, had introduced Joan Baez to the American music public.[39] The folk festival, though, had not been held in 1961 and 1962. But sometime in 1961 Bill received a letter from Pete Seeger and Theo Bikel asking him to join the board of directors of the reconstituted event. Bill believes that Pete's interest in him had stemmed from a meeting that the two had back in 1957 in Philadelphia, during Bill's one-semester residence at the Wharton School of Business. Meeting Seeger backstage at one of his concerts, the two had talked about Woody Guthrie and Bill's songbook. Of course, Pete surely would have known, too, about the close friendship between his little brother Mike and Bill.

Although presence on the Newport board of directors was clearly a financial and time-consuming burden for Bill, requiring several uncompensated trips to New York, he nevertheless agreed to membership because of the opportunity to promote the cause of old-time music and bluegrass at the festival. The festival was designed as a nonprofit affair run by musicians; all performers, professional and amateur, would be paid fifty dollars plus expenses. Seeger and Bikel, particularly, saw the festival as a means of paying tribute and giving exposure to the grassroots musicians from whom the professionals had learned. Bill welcomed the opportunity to be a passionate spokesman for the music he had loved all his life, and, in addition to bringing such bluegrass greats as Bill Monroe, Mac Wiseman, and Jim and Jesse to the festival, was delighted to present old heroes like Wiley and Zeke Morris and Dorsey Dixon to the Newport audience. Bill participated actively in the festival's planning and also acted as master of ceremonies during the old-time music segments; as well, he was the host of a panel on bluegrass music designed to touch upon the music's origins and both its old-time and progressive elements. The panel consisted of Bill Monroe, Mike Seeger, Eric Weissberg, Jim and Jesse, Mac Wiseman, Ralph Rinzler, and the Morris Brothers.

Although he had not been initially responsible for his inclusion, Bill was particularly pleased with the appearance of Mississippi John Hurt at the festival. Mississippi John, a superb singer and finger-style guitarist who had recorded in the late twenties, had only recently (in March 1963) been "rediscovered" in Avalon, Mississippi, by Thomas Hoskins, on the strength of the clues presented by Hurt's 1928 recording of "Avalon Blues." Only a few months after his discovery, Hurt electrified the Newport crowd with his gentle singing style and syncopated guitar picking, and against George Wein's policy, he was called back for an encore. Mac Wiseman, who was scheduled to appear immediately after Mississippi John, recognized that he had been upstaged but nevertheless accepted the delay with respect and good humor.

In a sense, Newport was Bill's swan song in the United States. The festival had been both frustrating and rewarding, but no less so than his relationship with Abbott, Proctor, and Paine. He had gone through training in New York and had then spent two years in Charlottesville as a registered representative of the New York Stock Exchange. His association, though, was conditional: he was asked to stop playing music professionally and to cease all recording. The firm had postponed enforcement of this policy, however, because of Bill's contract with Starday. The contract called for the recording of at least three more LPs. It was clear, though, that Bill did not like the stock business anyway, and these stipulations only confirmed his decision to resign. When the NYSE reconsidered its policy, Bill replied that it was too late: "I'm going to England."

Before Bill moved abroad in October 1963, he recorded a large body of songs for Starday at Wynwood Studio, Pete Kuykendall's operation in Falls Church, Virginia. Born on January 15, 1938, in Washington, D.C., Kuykendall was a record collector, discographer, radio personality, and bluegrass musician who in 1966 became a co-founder of *Bluegrass Unlimited*, the premiere magazine of bluegrass music. He had a longstanding interest in the technology of music as well, having studied at Capitol Radio and Electronics Institute in Washington, and had worked as a recording division technician at the Library of Congress. He was also experienced in the recording of bluegrass musicians, having engineered the Country Gentlemen's second LP for Folkways (the first had been produced by Mike Seeger). By the time Bill Clifton availed himself of his services, Kuykendall had built a state-of-the-art recording studio in the basement of his home in Falls Church, Virginia, and had overseen the recording of many notable musicians, including Mississippi John Hurt.

The recordings in Kuykendall's studio also inaugurated a fruitful relationship between Bill and the Country Gentlemen. The Gentlemen were the premiere progressive bluegrass band in America, valued not only for their musicianship but also for their eclectic choice of songs. They were capable of moving freely from the traditional styles of bluegrass to the experimental sounds of jazz and rock and roll, and became one of the first bluegrass bands to record some Bob Dylan songs. Universally acknowledged as the first "progressive" band, primarily because of their willingness to utilize songs from any musical genre, the Country Gentlemen nevertheless built a very comfortable rapport with Bill and easily adjusted to the old-time songs he favored. They appeared on Bill's last American recording sessions and toured with him frequently during the last months of 1963 before he moved to England.

In a sense, Bill's relationship with the Country Gentlemen had begun back in 1958, when Johnny Clark told him about "a kid from Maryland" he had heard on WARL in Arlington who sang with a sky-high tenor and played an inventive and fiery style of mandolin. This was John Duffey. When Bill contacted Duffey by phone, he found that the young musician had been much influenced by Bill's recording of "Mary Dear" and had in fact been encouraged to take up the mandolin after hearing that instrument on the song.

John Humbird Duffey Jr. was born on March 4, 1934 in Washington, D.C. He attended Bethesda–Chevy Chase High School in Washington and as a teenager became attracted to the bluegrass music he heard on local radio. His father, who had been a singer in the Metropolitan Opera, had no affection for country music but nevertheless contributed to his son's success in that realm by teaching him how to breathe properly when he sang. Duffey became one of the most powerful singers in bluegrass music, with a voice that could take flight or modulate into a breathy vibrato. Duffey performed in a variety of groups but gained prominence after 1957 with the most famous and influential version of the Country Gentlemen, the group that included Charlie Waller (guitar), Eddie Adcock (banjo), and Tom Gray (bass). Each of these individuals was a first-rate musician, but Tom Gray, who had joined Bill Clifton on some of his recordings in 1959, was acknowledged as the finest bass player in bluegrass music. With his continuous pattern of dynamic, rolling chords, Gray clearly revealed, and freely acknowledged, his indebtedness to George Shuffler. Gray's association with Clifton continued, off and on, well into the first decade of the twenty-first century.[40]

Although this was the "classic" Country Gentlemen band that did most to define the "progressive bluegrass" sound, the group actually won its initial fame in the folk revival in 1960, when Mike Seeger produced an album for them on the Folkways label (*Country Songs, Old and New*). Duffey and his partners deliberately began learning traditional songs by listening to old 78 rpm hillbilly records and to material archived in the Library of Congress in order to satisfy the hunger of their newfound folk music fans. With their receptivity to old songs, they were uniquely prepared to play with Bill Clifton.

Bill was only a few years older than the Gentlemen, but they seem to have treated him almost as an elder statesman. They certainly respected him but also may have found him a bit overly formal and dignified. Consequently, they liked to play practical jokes on him. The Gentlemen's humor was not nearly as sophisticated as their music. John Duffey, whose humor could never be accused of subtlety, seems to have been the purveyor of most of the "jokes" pulled by the Gentlemen. A handful of stories have survived concerning their dealings with Bill and of the hijinks of their days on the road. Back in the days before the postal service became acutely concerned about the content of mailings, Duffey supposedly sent Bill a greasy letter, containing a few turkey scraps, a few days after Thanksgiving, saying "I know that you like the turkey skin best of all." On the occasions when he was not participating in the driving, Bill often sat in the back seat of their touring car and slept. On at least one occasion, Duffey piled a cluster of beer and whiskey bottles next to the door on the side where Bill was sleeping, and then stopped the car at a corner where a couple of older ladies were standing. When Bill opened the door to get out, the bottles clattered to the pavement near the women's feet, and a flustered Bill tried hard to act nonchalant. Much more innocent were the incidents designed to combat the boredom of the road. More than one gullible waitress in a late-night greasy-spoon café was assured by Duffey or Waller that Bill was the leader of the Kingston Trio or was some other famous music personality.

Bill and the Gentlemen toured widely on the East Coast through much of 1962 and 1963, playing throughout New England and in Virginia, Maryland, Pennsylvania, Ohio, and West Virginia. Except for appearances in Virginia, they apparently made no excursions into the South. If the Country Gentlemen harbored any reservations or resentments about being billed as virtually the sidemen for Bill Clifton, they never expressed such feelings. The two surviving members of the Gentlemen, Eddie Adcock and Tom

Gray, instead still speak with awe about Bill and about the knowledge and skill he brought to the music. All four of the Gentlemen had grown up with his music and were honored with the privilege of playing with him. Bill, on the other hand, was grateful to have the support of one of the greatest bands in country music history and must have been pleased with the youthful audience they attracted to his shows.

The Country Gentlemen also helped Bill fulfill the recording obligations owed to Don Pierce. These recordings had commenced back in early September 1962, when only two of the Gentlemen, John Duffey and Tom Gray, were playing with him. They were joined by Paul Craft, Mike Seeger, Curtis Lee, and Carl Nelson at Pete Kuykendall's Wynwood Studio. They recorded seventeen songs, two of which were unissued. These recordings became the basis of an album about war and patriotism, called *Soldier, Sing Me a Song* (Starday 213). Projecting no particular ideological bent, but perhaps reflecting the gradual buildup of our military involvement in Vietnam, the album presented a wide variety of songs that commented on our wars, from the War of 1812 to World War II and the Cold War. Paul Clayton was listed as writer or co-writer of six of the songs. Bill even managed to work in a tribute to his own branch of the service, an instrumental version of "The Marine's Hymn."

On August 5, 6, and 7, 1963, Bill recorded again at Wynwood, this time with the backing of the entire Country Gentlemen unit plus Mike Seeger and the fiddling Justice Brothers (Paul and Roy). The same group recorded again on September 3 and 4, 1963. The accumulated cuts appeared on *Code of the Mountains* (Starday SLP 271) and *Bluegrass in the American Tradition* (Nashville NLP 2018). Some of the songs also appeared later on an LP in England, *Mountain Ramblings*. In 1975 thirty-six songs from these 1963 sessions appeared on a two-LP album, called *Going Back to Dixie*, produced by the Bear Family label in Germany.

This ambitious project, while musically superb, tells us much about Bill Clifton's vision—and version—of the music he loved. In the cover art and liner notes that accompany *Going Back to Dixie* one finds a labored attempt to affix a dubious theme to a wide assortment of old songs. His romantic fascination with Appalachian life and culture, and his attempt to link his personal music to such beginnings, are strongly displayed.[41] The album's front and back covers set the stage for this illusion by depicting Bill as a mountain man returning from a long hunt, carrying a rifle in one hand and a guitar slung across his back. He is being greeted by his wife and small children standing outside a rude cabin (it was actually Paul Clayton's cabin). The liner notes similarly portray the songs as unique expressions of mountain life, depicting customs or practices that were widely popular in the Appalachians. While some songs in the collection—such as "Ground Hog Hunt" or "Jim Hatfield's Son"—may have had a mountain provenance or theme, the great majority of them are instead generically Southern rural in theme and were the products not of mountain musicians but of contemporary country songwriters and Tin Pan Alley or Blackface minstrel composers. The album's title cut, "Going Back to Dixie," for example, described by Bill as the expression of a mountain boy's determination to leave the northern factory where he unhappily works, and to return to the "old plantation where the cotton blossoms grow," is typical of the plethora of songs that profit from the nostalgic power of the romantic South.

The most famous song to come out of these sessions had nothing to do with Dixie or the mountains but instead built upon the venerable urban legend of the Vanishing Hitchhiker, in this case a little girl who continued to reappear each year on the anniversary of her death in an automobile accident. Don Pierce had sent Bill a poem based on the story, and while Bill liked the tale, he did not like its melody. He then asked John Duffey to come up with a suitable and singable tune. "Bringing Mary Home" went on to become one of bluegrass music's classic and enduring songs.

With these recording obligations resolved, Bill completed preparations for his and the family's move to England. While the Marburg love of travel played a role in his decision, his desire to abandon the unhappy life of a stockbroker, while also reducing the influence of his father, played a far more critical role in his decision to live abroad. Above all, he was ready to pursue music full time. He understood that he had a coterie of fans in England and had cheerfully corresponded with many of them. He had also ranked high in the popularity polls conducted by some of the small British country music journals. *Country and Western Express*, for example, ran polls from 1958 to 1963 that showed him ranking consistently as number one or in the top-ten listings for the categories of "Favorite Male Performers" and "Favorite Bluegrass Performers."[42] Don Pierce had done his job well in placing Bill's Mercury and Starday products in the hands of English merchandizers. Bill told historian Nathan Gibson, "I wouldn't have been able to move if Don hadn't gotten there first." Pierce had made a trip around the world in 1959 or 1960, calling on record merchandizers in the British Isles, the European continent, and Japan. He held a dinner party in Soho to which most British music industry people were invited. Pierce succeeded in placing Starday records with London, Melodisc, and other labels. Particularly influential were Bill's recordings of "Mary Dear," "Lonely Heart Blues," "Little White Washed Chimney," and "My Old Pal of Yesterday," released in England in 1958 on a Mercury EP, MEP 9546 (a 45 rpm disc that contained four songs). While other Bill Clifton songs were released on British labels, either by Bill alone or on compilation discs, *The Carter Family Memorial Album*, released on the London label in 1962, was the item that seems to have had the greatest impact on English country music enthusiasts and collectors.

A few months before Bill made his actual move, he made a financial decision that ultimately complicated his life in England: he bought a house in which to store the furniture and personal items from his rented Glen Echo home. Not then knowing how long his English sojourn would last, he asked Jack Schwab, a close friend and developer, to build him a home with surrounding acreage on a site Schwab was developing near Charlottesville. Bill says, "I didn't know how much pain it would cause in the years that lay ahead." He borrowed $10,000 from a bank in Baltimore for the down payment and asked a law office in Charlottesville to keep his checkbook and to pay the loan interest and his American Express bills each month. He rented the house to some young women who were attending nursing school at the University of Virginia, and left behind his furniture, china, and silverware, and some personal items such as a Weymann five-string banjo and a twelve-gauge shotgun. Bill was a very trusting individual! The rental sum was enough to cover all the expenses that required payment each month. Probably overly confident that his American obligations were secure, Bill obtained passports for himself and his family, and booked passage on a ship to England.

3

TAKING OLD-TIME MUSIC TO
ENGLAND, 1963–1970

American country music was certainly not unknown in England before Bill Clifton arrived in 1963. A small but knowledgeable and enthusiastic community of fans and musicians were well aware of the music made by American country and bluegrass musicians. Hillbilly records in fact had arrived in the 1920s, soon after they were first produced in the United States, and were reissued on as many as twenty-five labels, such as Regal, Regal-Zonophone, Decca, Parlophone, and Panachord. Panachord, preeminently, issued several hundred discs that featured music from such American labels as Brunswick and American ARC. British merchandisers, however, were rather discriminating in their choices. Many hillbilly performers never saw their records released in the United Kingdom. Carter Family material, for example, was not reissued in England, nor was most of the backwoods fare featured in American record catalogues. Jimmie Rodgers's records, on the other hand, circulated extensively, as they did in many parts of the world, such as India, Australia, New Zealand, and Africa. In Tony Russell's view, "hillbilly songs were valued not for the regional or stylistic idiosyncrasies of their performers, or for the particular musical devices they embodied, but for what they seemed to reveal of a mythical America." Above all, the American cowboy mystique tended to color the marketing decisions made by British record producers and promoters. Cowboy singers and yodelers proved enduringly popular. Speaking of today's British country music scene, Russell said, "The myth lingers. The campfires still burn; the shots still ring out in the streets of Tombstone."[1]

Cowboy consciousness certainly affected the reception given to Carson Robison when he toured in the United Kingdom in 1932, the first American "hillbilly" to take his music to England. The Kansas-born Robison was capable of performing and writing cowboy songs, such as "Carry Me Back to the Lone Prairie"—he could supply anything that the market demanded—but his talents were much more varied than that. He provided guitar accompaniment for Wendell Hall, Vernon Dalhart, and other singers as early as 1924; he whistled on a number of recordings; he sang duets with people like Frank Luther; and he was country music's earliest independent songwriter, specializing particularly in "event" songs (topical songs about train wrecks, murders, and similar material). He was still going strong as late as 1957, when he recorded a very popular comic recitation called "Life Gets Teejus" (tedious). But in England, Robison and his band, the Pioneers, were treated as minstrels of the West, cowboys who had learned their ballads around a campfire or in the bunkhouse. During his six-month tour in England (the first of at least three that he made in that country), Robison gave numerous concerts, appeared in film shorts, consented to interviews, and recorded a number of radio shows for Radio Luxembourg, the commercial continental station that boomed its broadcasts into the British Isles. On those broadcasts Robison's band was known as the Oxydol Cowboys, named for the popular detergent that sponsored them.[2]

Another wave of interest in American country music came in the mid-1950s, when such expatriates as Alan Lomax and Rambling Jack Elliott took up residence in England and began transplanting their favorite versions of American country songs and ballads. Lomax, who was based in London from 1950 to 1958, was an indefatigable promoter of American and British musicians, and a collector of folk songs throughout the Continent and elsewhere. He was also active as a host on BBC, where he featured the music of people like Jean Ritchie, Burl Ives, Peggy Seeger, and the Mountain Ramblers, a bluegrass band from Galax, Virginia. With the assistance of Peggy Seeger, he also compiled a guitar instruction book, *American Folk Guitar*, which included a sketchy introduction to Maybelle Carter's style, an incentive for musicians and fans to sample more thoroughly the Carter Family's music.[3] Elliott, on the other hand, relishing his role as an itinerant cowboy, went to England in 1955 and gave numerous concerts throughout the British Isles, popularizing the music of Woody Guthrie and other country performers. A very young Mick Jagger bought his first guitar after hearing Elliott busking on a London railroad platform.[4] Other young British musicians heard their first examples of American country music after 1955, when the English musician Lonnie Donegan, a former jazz musician, began experimenting with a version of string band jazz described as Skiffle. In the enthusiasm that followed Donegan's popular recording of "Rock Island Line"—a song taken from the repertory of African American songster Huddie "Leadbelly" Ledbetter—British fans and musicians became aware of "Wabash Cannon Ball," "Wreck of the Old 97," and other songs of country origin. Many Carter Family songs (although not always identified as such) became popular in England through the performances of the Skiffle bands. John Lennon's Quarrymen was only one of many Skiffle bands that appeared in the wake of Donegan's popularity.[5]

Many of the fans and collectors who communicated with Bill Clifton had first learned about country music through the records and broadcasts of Carson Robison, Jimmie Rodgers, and other pioneer American hillbillies. Dave Haxell, in fact, had attended some of Robison's concerts. Younger fans, like Dave Barnes, heard country music through the broadcasts of the American Armed Forces Network and began building their record collections largely through the purchase of British reissues. Knowing that recordings had a short shelf life, and that their favorites would not always be commercially available, Barnes, Haxell, and others also became involved in the network of record collectors that spanned the globe, and they began corresponding and exchanging material with people like John Edwards from Australia and Eugene Earle from the United States. In 1954 Haxell and George Tye published one of the first periodicals devoted to collecting, *The Hillbilly-Folk Record Journal*. From 1957 to 1964 Dave Barnes also compiled a small record journal, *Country and Western Record Review*, and managed to make connections with every commercial record dealer in England. Barnes, Haxell, and other fans of old-time country music were well aware of Bill Clifton's music, such as his widely circulated Mercury EP (four songs) of 1958, and had given him a great deal of publicity in their journals, where he typically ranked high in the popularity polls. The Canadian-born Murray Kash, who was a pioneering country disc jockey on BBC, had also played Bill's versions of "Blue Ridge Mountain Blues" and other songs on his show. English country music fans were delighted, then, when they learned in late 1963 that Bill had decided to make an extended visit to the British Isles.[6]

Bill and family arrived in England on the *USS Bremen* in late October 1963. The Marburgs now numbered seven; Sara Lee had given birth to two more daughters, Chandler and Cameron. Expecting to be there only a couple of months, while he tested the commercial appeal of his music, Bill applied for a residence permit and never seriously considered seeking British citizenship. His goals, however, were very ambitious. An item in the December 7, 1963, issue of *Billboard* magazine announced that "Bill Clifton, well known country music artist, has arrived in Great Britain on the first leg of a world tour which will span five continents and 27 countries" (another newspaper account, from Fredericksburg, Virginia, spoke of thirty-seven countries). The *Billboard* announcement also mentioned upcoming television and BBC appearances, and projected shows in South Africa, India, and Japan—and Bill didn't even have an agent yet.

Commercial acclaim, however, would have to wait. Bill first needed to find a place to stay. With the assistance of George Haxell, who met the Marburg family at the dock, Bill set out to find a temporary residence. Driving with his family in a previously purchased and reserved Volkswagen bus, and laboring to master the unfamiliar roads and driving style of England, Bill followed Haxell and his companion on a harrowing drive that took him through downtown London and on to Leigh-on-Sea in southeastern England. There, the family found a bed-and-breakfast where they lived for about ten days while looking for a more permanent home. With his family firmly in support of his decision, Bill began looking for rental property and for adequate schools for his three older children. Any reservations Bill and Sarah Lee might have had about taking their children into an uncertain school situation were tempered by the knowledge that educational conditions back home were in complete disarray. Faced with the threat of racial desegregation, Virginia had closed its public schools. The Marburgs were more than content with the educational options and advantages that they found in southeast England.

The family lived in a couple of homes before eventually settling into a three-story stone cottage (called Stone Oak) in Sevenoaks, a small community located on one of the principal commuter rail lines in western Kent, in southeast England, about twenty-eight miles from London. The town's principal claims to fame were Knole Park, a thousand-acre park filled with "millions of trees," and the fact that the revered English poet John Donne had been vicar there in the seventeenth century. Sevenoaks seemed to be the ideal place to live, a nice community with good schools[7] where the kids would feel secure, and with easy access to London. It remained the

Bill and Sarah Lee's children: from top to bottom, Tad, Streett, LeeLee, Chandler, Cameron, Grainger, and Rush. Courtesy of Mary Lynn Marburg Brett

Marburg home for the next four years. Bill quickly got to work running down leads about possible musical engagements. He did find immediate work in England, even if it was sometimes only teaching guitar lessons (Dave Barnes, in fact, was his first eager student). Fortunately, Don Pierce had done his job well in making available and publicizing Bill's records in

England, and all of his songs had been licensed for release on London and other Decca labels. By the end of December, through the recommendation of the Decca people, Bill had secured the management of the Patrick Robinson Agency and was advised to find a new song, preferably topical, that he could present immediately to the British public.[8] Robinson took Bill to Regent Sound, a low-budget studio on London's Denmark Street, where he recorded a song written by Geoff Stevens, a songwriter for Southern Music, who later became famous for "Winchester Cathedral." Few topics were hotter at that time than the Beatles, who had not yet gone to the United States but who were creating quite a stir in their personal appearances in England. Through his knowledge of Woody Guthrie's work, Bill was well aware of how effective the talking blues form could be in making humorous but biting statements of social commentary. Stevens came through with a talking blues tune about the fabulous foursome, "Beatle Crazy," which Bill recorded on the London label before the year ended. It wasn't the first song inspired by the Beatles; Dora Bryan's "All I Want for Christmas is a Beatle" seems to hold that distinction, but Bill's tune was a clever spoof. He performed the song in the whimsical, drawling style of a country boy who had come to Britain in his "rawhide jacket and ten-gallon hat" to find himself befuddled by the Beatles' fantastic popularity. As expected, the song commented on the long hair of the Beatles while noting that the narrator was losing his.

The song was decidedly out of character for Bill, but it garnered for him an immediate spate of favorable publicity and a wealth of public exposure. There is no evidence that the Beatles ever knew about the song (which in any case was only a gentle treatment of the group), but Bill did receive invitations to appear on BBC's *Tonight* show, ITV's (Independent Television) *Late Scene*, ABC's *Hullabaloo*, and BBC's *Juke Box Jury*. The publicity seemed to be an auspicious beginning for Bill's unfolding British musical career.[9]

As 1964 dawned, however, Bill learned that such media exposure would have only limited and short-lived effectiveness. Media attention, after all, had been sparked by the novelty of "Beatle Crazy" and not by the excellence of Bill's performing style. Neither Bill nor Pat Robinson was quite certain about how to market the young American singer. But following Robinson's suggestion, Bill capitulated to the English vogue for cowboy characters and began wearing a Stetson hat. While a small market for bluegrass and country music existed in England, England was also in the midst of a folk

Bill in a London television studio (UTV) during "Beatle Crazy" days. Courtesy of
Bill Clifton

music revival that was very much like that prevailing in the United States.
Thinking probably of the American success enjoyed by Peter, Paul, and Mary,
Robinson brought Bill into the studio with two folk singers, Dave Goulder
and Jacqui McShee, in the hopes of marketing a commercially attractive
trio. Unfortunately, Bill had contracted a severe sinus infection that he could
not shake off, and he felt that he was not at his best. Nevertheless, the trio
tested their voices and compatibility on a few songs like "Rambling Boy,"
which Bill had learned from its composer, Tom Paxton, at the Newport Folk
Festival, but they failed to generate enough interest to warrant a recording
contract. Goulder went on to success as a ballad singer, principally of railroad songs, and McShee became the lead vocalist of an enduringly popular
trio called Pentangle. Although this was Bill's last serious venture as a "folk
singer," he did occasionally borrow songs from British folk revivalists. For
example, when he made a brief trip to the United States in July 1965, he
visited Wynwood Studio and, along with John Duffey, Eddie Adcock, and
Tom Gray, recorded four songs that came directly from Dave Goulder and
other British folk singers. He also performed at folk festivals and folk clubs

with such veteran musicians as Goulder, Martin Carthey, Bob Davenport, and Fred Jordan, a marvelous traditional ballad singer from Ludlow. A few years later, in 1966, Bill even hosted an hour-long variety program on BBC called *Cellar Full of Folk*, which ran until April 1967. The program was broadcast at 3 P.M. from the Playhouse Theatre in London, not far from the Charing Cross Railway station Bill used on his commutes from Sevenoaks. While Bill seldom deviated from the old-time country songs he had favored all his life, his guests, for the most part, tended to be musicians and singers who were currently active in the folk revival. A local bluegrass band, the Echo Mountain Boys, however, did play on at least one show in 1967, presenting such traditional American country songs as "Little Birdie" and "Dream of the Miner's Child." The show's producers at first insisted that the program be scripted, but Bill wanted more spontaneity and excitement, and so he persuaded them to let the program run live. Predictably, a song sometimes proved to be in the wrong key, or an instrument was out of tune in the first live programs, but the performers discovered that no one particularly cared when they started over again. Bill received a good deal of satisfaction from hosting and playing on this show, but he had already learned that a country music career in England could be sustained only through useful contacts, hard disciplined work, and constant travel, a regimen destined, unfortunately, to place severe strains on his marriage and family life.

Bill solved the travel problem through the purchase of a Dennis Diesel Coach, a hardy, forty-six-passenger bus that had seen public service in the 1930s and had been refurbished in the 1940s. The bus had more recently

Bill with the Echo Mountain Boys (in Germany), late 1960s. Courtesy of Bill Clifton

Bill with his Dennis Diesel bus (returning from a trip to the European continent), mid-1960s. Courtesy of Bill Clifton

been owned by a family of migrant workers (a woman and her children) who lived and traveled in it in their quest for part-time work. The bus moved only with great difficulty, had one working brake, and carried only used tires. Fortunately, Bill found a mechanic—Alex Guest—who rebuilt the vehicle, removed the seats, and added sleeping bunks, a kitchen area, and a toilet. Guest was a country music fan and journalist who worked with George Haxell and George Tye, chauffeuring them to their meetings and assisting them with the editing and publishing of their journal. Guest and another mechanic, Leslie Smith, not only kept the diesel bus running but also worked on the other automobiles Bill purchased from time to time, making sure that they passed the apparently lax English inspection requirements (on one occasion, Guest left one of Bill's cars for inspection, placed a small branch on top of one of the tires, and returned to find the car approved but the twig still there!).

Guest was part of that small network of friends and country music enthusiasts who befriended Bill through journal publicity, booking contacts, and other promotional endeavors. They all felt blessed to have Bill in their presence and could easily agree with John Atkins, who declared that Bill was a "walking encyclopedia of country music history." Atkins, an accountant by trade, was particularly impressed by the fact that Bill had not only mastered much of the Carter Family's repertory, but he had also known all three members of the Carter trio. Like Haxell and Tye, Barnes was the editor of a country music magazine, *Country and Western Record Review*, and he had long known and liked Bill's music. Barnes had first become attracted to American country music as a teenager, but he soon began to associate this music with the cowboy characters he saw and heard in traveling circuses. In 1951 he began to buy 78 rpm records, first those he heard in cowboy movies and then those of a more general country nature. This hobby brought him in contact with Haxell's and Tye's *Hillbilly-Folk Record Journal*, which in turn introduced him to the world of record collectors. Barnes made his living working with his father in the business of repairing and reselling art pieces. Although Barnes was a resident of Dover, his business required a commuter-train trip each day to London, about seventy-six miles away. While making his living in the art business, Barnes compiled one of the largest collections of country records in the world, an avocation that he eventually turned into a thriving archive called the British Academy of Country Music, complete with the production and marketing of commercial reissues. When Don Pierce made his earlier visits to England, Barnes took him around the country to visit all of the record dealers.

Two other country music enthusiasts, Robert Ronald and Jim Marshall, had first become aware of Bill Clifton through the Mercury and Starday records released in England (on both anthologies and solo LPs). Ronald, a collector of traditional country music, came to country music in 1956 through an interest in Johnny Cash. A couple of years later he heard one of Bill's EPs and was impressed by his clarity of tone, enunciation, and choice of songs. This musical interest was joined later by a strong personal interest in Bill as a man, when Ronald found out that Bill was endlessly patient in his willingness to answer questions and discuss the history of country music. Through his book store, Ronald sold Bill's records and famous songbook, and eventually compiled the first and most complete discography of his music that had ever been assembled.

Along with Mike Storey, Jim Marshall created a circulating audio journal called *Folk Voice*, a five-inch reel-to-reel tape consisting of short essays, interviews, and reviews that subscribers heard and then passed on to others. Storey and Marshall eventually compiled more than sixty issues and were very eclectic in their music coverage, including material on British and American folk singers and both old-time and contemporary country-and-western musicians. The journal existed from 1960 to 1972 and was circulated in the United States by Herb and Helene Wolf, who worked out of their home in the Bronx, New York. From time to time, *Folk Voice* sponsored festivals or concerts in London at the Cecil Sharp House (named for the great folk dance and folk song collector of the early twentieth century), and Marshall booked Bill into various folk clubs, including his own, the Stanford Arms in Brighton.[10]

The folk clubs, which seem to have been a peculiarly English contribution to the folk revival, proved to be Bill's commercial salvation. These clubs had existed at least since the early fifties, when Ewan MacColl established his Ballads and Blues Club, but their numbers proliferated during the revival of the sixties. John Atkins, a country music journalist who owned his own club, guessed that there may have been fifty clubs when Bill arrived, and more than five hundred when he left for the Philippines only a few years later. Although the regimen was difficult, Bill found that he could make a living playing in these intimate venues. At first, the pay for an evening's performance was about ten pounds, the equivalent of fifty dollars in American money. Bill initially played one or two clubs a week, but within a year he was playing five or six days a week. Held in small, smoke-filled rooms, usually in a space set aside in a pub and often without a stage or electrical amplification, the clubs typically attracted fifty to a hundred ardent fans (although Bill remembers one club in Liverpool that seated two thousand). Most club concerts were amateur affairs that were open to anyone who wanted to sing a song, although guest "professionals" were often featured. Bill's first folk club gig was a show in Nottingham arranged by Reg Cooper, a singer and telephone switchboard operator who was legally blind. Unlike most of the similar venues, this particular folk club actually had a small stage.[11]

Bill was impressed by the decorum of the British audiences and by the seriousness with which they approached his music. Listeners in the United States had never been so respectful of his music, nor had they listened with the kind of silence and attention that he now encountered. He was particularly pleased that he could present a bit of history or commentary concerning the songs he performed. Bill recalls that he "was standing with the audience, most of the time, and trying to sing to the back of the room." He in fact felt an intimacy that was rare in any other setting. Singing usually without the benefit of any sound amplification (and generally without other instrumental support), he had to be strong and articulate.

Guitar accompaniment seems to have been rather rare in the folk clubs, and Bill's style, particularly his rhythm, made an immediate positive impression. John Atkins said that "Bill's guitar style was incredibly advanced to the English ear." Another English musician and folk club regular, the banjo player Laurence Diehl, averred that Bill was a "great rhythm player. Playing with him felt like a freight train was on stage with you."[12] Many years later another British folk musician, Brian Bull, could still remember, almost with a sense of awe, a "neat trick" Bill used in order to amplify the sound of his guitar: his tendency to raise the instrument so that its sound hole lined up with the microphone, and then to lower it when he resumed singing. This practice was actually commonplace among American bluegrass guitar players, who sought to amplify the sound of their instrument while executing a guitar run, or to achieve a dynamic visual effect, but Bull maintained that he had never seen anyone else do it.[13] On the other hand, Bill felt that the guitar was a bit limiting and that he needed something to relieve the instrument's potential monotony. Consequently, he began featuring the autoharp in all of his concerts, using the style popularized by Maybelle Carter. Although he played the autoharp throughout his years in England, he later argued that his faith in the instrument was particularly affirmed after 1970, when the celebrated American luthier, Tom Morgan, made him one that he played for the rest of his performing career.[14]

Diehl and Bull were only two of the many English musicians who profited from the presence of Bill Clifton. Bill's influence began to be felt almost as soon as he arrived in England in late 1963. In early December a note about his arrival appeared in a Sevenoaks newspaper and was read by Mrs. Brian Townend, whose husband taught the classics and was music director at the local high school. Along with two of her sons she visited Bill at his home and told him that her husband utilized bluegrass music in his classes, and that her sons had in fact organized a bluegrass band.

Brian "Fuzz" Townend encouraged his sons to play music, and one of them, Rick, embraced bluegrass after hearing an American band, the Mountain Ramblers from Galax, Virginia, play on a BBC show hosted by Alan Lomax. Rick listened to records by the Stanley Brothers and Pete Sayers (a pioneering British bluegrass musician) and studied Pete Seeger's famous book, *How to Play the Five-String Banjo*, but he had been particularly

Tom and Mary Morgan. Mary is holding an autoharp, one of the many fine instruments that Tom crafted. Courtesy of Tom Morgan

impressed by Bill's Carter Family tribute. Rick Townend later said that Bill's moving to Sevenoaks was "quite simply an amazing stroke of luck for the budding band." When Bill offered to tutor the Townend boys, who along with a few musical friends had named themselves the Echo Mountain Boys—named for a local hill called Echo Mount—they eagerly embraced this bit of good luck.[15] Almost every week, Bill spent several hours with them, gave them instruments and records, and soon decided that they were good enough to play with him.

The opportunity to utilize their support came in May 1964, when Bill and the boys played at a concert at the Sevenoaks school. In October they traveled to a Folk Voice Convention, sponsored by *Folk Voice*, the circulating tape-recording magazine. By July 17, 1965, Bill had become sufficiently impressed by the Echo Mountain Boys' talents to invite them to play with him at a festival in Keele. In a sense, the American folk music revival was only now beginning to demonstrate its effects on the British folk scene, and Bill's participation at the Newport Folk Festival in 1963 was well known in English folk circles. Held on the university campus, Keele became the British equivalent of Newport and eventually became the setting for the National Folk Festival. From its inception, the three-day

Bill, with three children (Streett, Lee Lee, and Chandler), standing in front of the Dennis Diesel bus, England, 1964. Courtesy of Chandler Marburg

festival had a "distinctly purist air" about it and was generally prone to favoring traditional musicians over popular ones.[16]

Only two weeks later, on July 31, 1965, Bill and the Echo Mountain Boys played at a large festival in Cambridge headlined by the popular Irish group, the Clancy Brothers and Tommy Makem. Bill had only recently returned from the United States, bearing gifts for Rick and Andy Townend, their first professional-quality banjo and mandolin (built by Tom Morgan). Promoted largely by Labor Party activists, such as firefighter Ken Woolard, who had been inspired by a film about the Newport Jazz Festival, the Cambridge festival nevertheless opened its roster to a wide array of musicians; Bill and Hedy West, for example, were booked because they were perceived to be "wonderful characters, not left wing necessarily, but socially aware. Their music was about something." Attracting about fourteen hundred people, the festival was also unique because it marked one of the earliest appearances in Europe of Paul Simon (listed in the program as "Simons") and also because on Sunday morning U.S. Air Force Sergeant Fred Moody conducted a session that was described as a fundamentalist "folk religious service" in "country and western style." This America-centric feature seems not to have been repeated in later festivals at Cambridge.[17] Bill returned to the festival the following year and was thrilled to play alongside the great American guitarist and singer Arthel "Doc" Watson, from Deep Gap, North Carolina, who had traveled to England with his son, Merle. Watson's appearance marked the beginning of a continuous stream of American traditional singers who appeared over the years at English folk venues.

Although Bill and the Boys traveled all over England in his big Dennis Diesel bus, their most prestigious concert was presented in London on February 5, 1966, at the venerable Royal Albert Hall (opened in 1871 by Queen Victoria as a dedication to her husband, Prince Albert). The concert was sponsored by Elektra Records, an American company that hoped to profit from the emerging revival in England, and booked by Roy Guest, a Turkish-born music entrepreneur who promoted the London concerts of some very important performers such as Simon and Garfunkel and the Incredible String Band. The Royal Albert Hall concert attracted about seventy-two hundred people. In addition to Bill and the Echo Mountain Boys (who were all teenagers at the time), the concert included some popular English groups such as the Dubliners and the Ian Campbell Folk Group, and the Americans, Hedy West and Tom Paxton. The event marked the first time that American bluegrass musicians had been booked in the prestigious concert hall, and it must have seemed a partial fulfillment of Bill's dream, expressed in the concert program, to present bluegrass and folk music to an international audience.[18]

Bill did not simply make music in England, he also worked tirelessly to bring American country and bluegrass musicians to that country and to the European continent. Mike Seeger was particularly delighted to come because his first tour, in January 1965, introduced him to a new audience and enabled him to be reunited with his sister Peggy and her husband, Ewan MacColl (Peggy had been living in England since 1956). Bill noted that this trip "created an appetite for travel that continued throughout the rest of Mike's life."[19] Bill traveled with Mike to numerous towns and villages all over the country. Moving from town to town and negotiating the small and unfamiliar roads, the tour was grueling in and of itself, but it was rendered even more difficult by Mike's refusal to leave his instruments in the bus when they stopped to relax or eat in a pub. The musically eclectic Seeger traveled with many instruments, and he insisted on taking all of them inside at each stop. When Bill complained about the inconvenience and noted that Mike's brother Pete was not nearly so careful, Mike replied "Pete loses a lot of instruments."[20] In September 1965, Bill lent his Dennis Diesel to Mike and his musical buddies, John Cohen and Tracy Schwarz, who toured as the New Lost City Ramblers, playing eighteen engagements during a three-week stint, in towns small and large. John Cohen remembered the folk clubs where they played, saying that "small halls were what England was about. Little tiny towns and a pub . . . people standing around in their overcoats drinking their pints and singing—that was the ambiance."[21]

Bill was also involved, to varying degrees, with the British appearances of several American bluegrass musicians, such as the Stanley Brothers, Bill Monroe and the Blue Grass Boys, and Pete Kuykendall. The Stanleys visited England on March 11, 1966, appearing at Royal Albert Hall, and then continued their three-week tour with trips to Denmark, Switzerland, Sweden, and Germany. Bill remembers this tour with great affection and poignance, for it was the last time he saw Carter Stanley, who died on December 1, 1966. Bill took particular pride in the appearance of Bill Monroe, who was receiving belated recognition as the father of bluegrass music but who until this time had never presented a European concert. Bill did not book Monroe's shows, but he worked closely with Monroe's manager, Ralph Rinzler, to find appropriate dates and audiences for the bluegrass patriarch. Rinzler, a self-taught folklorist and bluegrass mandolin player

Doc Watson, Ralph Rinzler, and Bill Clifton (in England, 1967). Courtesy of John Atkins

from Passaic, New Jersey, had been working hard to revitalize Monroe's career and to demonstrate the vital role Monroe had played in American musical culture. Bill put Monroe up in his home, hosted a picking party for him in his garden, provided his bus and a driver for Monroe's tour, and opened for the bluegrass legend on a few occasions. The high point for Monroe came with his concert at Royal Albert Hall on June 10, 1966, where he was supported by the music of Bill Clifton and Hedy West. Monroe's 1966 performances provided a vital spark for fledgling English bluegrass musicians, and at least two of them, Dave Cousins and Ian McCann, left awestruck recollections of Monroe and his talented musicians, such as guitarist Peter Rowan and fiddler Richard Greene. McCann was certainly not alone in remembering the Royal Albert Hall event as an "unforgettable" and "hugely formative experience."[22]

Bill also brought the multi-talented Pete Kuykendall to England in 1966. Pete and Bill played at some of the requisite folk clubs but added a new, and not altogether pleasant, ingredient to Bill's performance career: a string of shows at military bases in England, Belgium, and Germany.[23] Pete and Bill were pleased to play their patriotic part in bolstering the morale of American soldiers, but the experience was otherwise frustrating and grueling. With Bill on the guitar and autoharp, and Pete playing mandolin and fiddle, the duo managed to find additional accompanying instrumentalists and appeared on as many as three bases per night. Driving at excessive speeds to get to the respective bases, this regimen did not leave the boys in very good shape, mentally or physically, to consistently present a first-rate show. Furthermore, the soldiers tended to be much more interested in drinking and finding hot dates than in listening to music. The experience was quite unlike anything that Bill had seen in the English folk clubs or at the festivals and parks in America. Of course, if he had been a veteran of the Texas honky-tonk scene, or of the bluegrass bars in cities like Cincinnati or Baltimore, he would have been very familiar with listeners who could be either lackluster or raucous.

Bill may not have realized it at the time, but this European excursion prepared him for a later phase of his career that came after 1970, when his English contacts began to dry up. During these years Bill made an extensive number of trips back home to visit his family or to participate in occasional recording sessions. He and his family also made a few vacation trips across the Channel in the years between 1963 and 1967, venturing as far south as Italy and as far east as the Soviet Union and Romania. Holland was a preferred destination because of its proximity, and a frequent location for musical performance. He and the Echo Mountain Boys presented concerts there in 1965 and 1966. An earlier trip to Switzerland in September 1964 resulted in an unexpected and informal recording session on the eighteenth of that month.

Bill had been invited to Zurich by a former high school classmate, William McCreery "Bill" Ramsey, who had been his roommate in 1947 at the Florida-Adirondack school but who had since become a successful pop and jazz singer in Germany. Sometimes described as "the man with the black voice" because of his soulful renditions of American pop songs, Ramsey claimed that Bill had introduced him to hillbilly music and had taught him how to play the guitar.[24] At a stop-off in Basel, Bill had wound up singing at a party of about thirty-five people held at the home of Werner Mueller but hosted by Charles "Chuck" Steiner, editor of a magazine called *Hillbilly*, and a long-time promoter of hillbilly music in Europe.

Steiner taped the evening's music on two microphones on a four-track home recording unit. Bill eventually gave permission for several of the songs to be issued on an LP. While agreeing to forego royalties, he stipulated that the record should not be issued as a professional product. Potential buyers, Bill believed, should not be misled about the quality of the record. The album cover should reflect the fact that the recording was a homemade product. Consequently, he refused to supply Steiner with a full-color professional photograph for the cover art. Instead, a local artist, Hans Geisen, drew the cover design showing a man walking down the road with a guitar slung over his shoulder. Although a road sign pointed toward Charlottesville, Virginia, the depicted scene, with its expansive vistas and semi-bleak landscape, was clearly a representation of the American West. Steiner eventually issued five hundred copies of the LP, which bore the title of *Wanderin'* (Hillbilly Records HR 5001).

Although the technical quality of the recordings is mediocre, it is nevertheless regrettable that the LP is out of print. The program presented by Bill is presumably the only aural evidence available of the kind of shows that he gave to folk clubs and similar venues. Supported mainly by his guitar, but with occasional autoharp interludes, Bill did a program of old-time songs introduced with spoken commentaries. He sang none of the "hit songs" from his Starday-Mercury years but instead concentrated primarily on traditional songs. He sang only two "modern" country songs, Hank Snow's "My Mother" and Lulu Belle and Scotty's "Remember Me." It is no surprise that Bill performed five Carter Family songs, including "Wildwood Flower," which long before had become a standard solo piece for country guitarists. He sang one Woody Guthrie song, "Ranger's Command," the great traditional ballad "John Henry," a music hall piece, "Little Girl Dressed in Blue" (which had been on the reverse side of "Beatle Crazy"), and the first commercial hillbilly hit from 1924, recorded many times by Vernon Dalhart, "The Prisoner's Song."

In the summer of 1967 Bill obtained passports for himself, Sarah Lee, the children, and an English au pair girl to assist as a babysitter, and set out across the Continent in his Dennis Diesel bus. He gave a few concerts, and the family camped out at various places. They used no credit cards but instead subsisted on the cash obtained from Bill's shows in England and on the Continent. One of his shows was a performance on Radio Denmark, presented at Tivoli Gardens in Copenhagen. The Clifton entourage crossed Sweden and Finland before entering the Soviet Union. They then made their way through Leningrad on the way to Moscow. Bill got fifty rubles for a one-hour show done for "the domestic circle" of Radio Moscow. While they drove through Russia, Ukraine, Romania, and Hungary, Bill listened to local music on his transistor radio and was impressed with the "folk music" he heard, thinking that it bore similarities to old-time American country music. For example, he speaks of hearing a female Russian singer who reminded him of the great American country singer Kitty

Bill, Sarah Lee, and the children (Sarah Lee holding baby Grainger), England, early 1960s. Courtesy of Chandler Marburg

Wells. He began to hatch the idea that the Russians might be ready to hear some visiting American act, if he could get State Department support and clearance. Bill Monroe, above all, became the center of his thinking. He had already spoken to Monroe about a possible trip to Russia, and Monroe had expressed some interest. When Bill Clifton told Mike Seeger about Monroe's agreement, the incredulous Seeger, knowing about the singer's rock-ribbed conservatism, said, "Does Bill know that Russia and the Soviet Union are the same place?!"

When he got back to England, Bill canceled a small tour to Devon and Cornwall, flew back to Washington, and had some talks with a few State Department functionaries. They told Bill that, because of the language barrier, they were skeptical that an American singer could find a receptive audience in Russia. They preferred to send dance troupes and Dixieland bands abroad. In retrospect, the State Department response seems ridiculous. Bill Monroe's music, and bluegrass in general, had already shown a remarkable ability to win the hearts and imaginations of non-English-speaking listeners around the world. One of Bill's questioners, the outgoing administrator of the Peace Corps in the Philippines, was apparently impressed by his demeanor, intelligence, and attitude, and asked him if he might be interested in taking on the position that he was vacating. Bill was tantalized by the idea, in part because of his love of adventure and hunger for travel. He also felt that the opportunity to work for the American government would be both a source of pride for his father and a way to thwart his efforts to lure him back to the United States.

Bill had already learned that the Baltimore bank was foreclosing on the $10,000 loan made to him for the Charlottesville house that he had built in order to store his furniture. Bill said, "That threw a monkey wrench into what was turning out to be exactly the musical career that I wanted in life." When his parents had visited Bill and family in England in the spring of 1966, his dad—who was on the board of the Baltimore bank holding Bill's mortgage—asked Bill how he was planning to pay back the money owed to the bank. When Bill said that he couldn't make the payment, his dad said that he would do so, on the condition that Bill would return to the United States and get a "real job." The Peace Corps opportunity presented that "real job," and Bill said, "I immediately saw it as an opportunity to satisfy my father's condition for repaying the $10,000 to the bank in Baltimore."

Bill's family, for the most part, was enthusiastic about the trip to the Philippines. Bill listed Mike Seeger as a reference. As expected, the FBI asked both Bill and Mike if Mike was related to Pete Seeger, a name that was notorious in State Department circles because of its association with left-wing politics. When Bill said yes, he was advised to take Mike's name off the list. Bill responded, "You can take *my* name off your list." "This stopped them dead in their tracks," he reported. Mike later told Bill that the FBI had similarly inquired about Bill's politics, and Seeger had assured them that Bill Clifton was apolitical. Bill then embarked on his new job as a government administrator.

Bill did one last gig at the Troubadour in London and then returned to the United States for a visit with his family and an intensive four-week language and culture course in Washington on Filipino dialects. Even though he could not learn the language, he continued with his newfound mission.

Somewhere in the Philippines, Bill, Sarah Lee, and the children, November 1969.
Courtesy of Chandler Marburg

After a three-day stay in Hawaii, where he met the volunteers, he gathered up his family and moved to the Philippines.

Despite the high hopes held by the Marburg family, who welcomed the chance to travel and find new adventures, the Peace Corps experience ultimately proved unsatisfactory. Bill had signed on for a three-year stint and was stationed initially at San Pablo in Luzon, about twenty-five miles southwest of Manila. Sarah Lee, though, did not like the location, and the kids had a difficult time adjusting in a place where customs were exotic and English-speaking friends were rare. One son, Streett, exhibited such strong resistance that he was permitted to go back to England, where he still lives. Tad claims to have "adjusted pretty well," but he also went back to England soon after Streett, presumably to provide companionship for his brother. Chandler had just begun first grade, but Bill and Sarah were dissatisfied with her educational situation, describing as "pedestrian training" the all-day instruction in English she received from an Italian nun. The nun apparently taught her students, most of whom knew no English at all, one word at a time on a daily basis. The teacher would say "door," and the students would repeat the word. The next day they would go on to something like "window." When asked what she learned at school, little Chandler said "door and window, and I already knew them!" The pace and quality of Chandler's education was probably only one factor that caused Sarah Lee's concern. But she begged Bill to transfer to Zamboanga, in Mindanao, where she had heard that a Peace Corps office was being vacated. Zamboanga was a much larger city, and the Peace Corps office was located only one hundred yards from the beach, a convenience that proved delightful to both Sarah Lee and the children.

Although Bill initially shared the idealism of the Peace Corps mission, his optimism soon flagged. He encountered many obstacles, both professional and personal. Bill liked the Filipino people and particularly enjoyed the coffee sessions that he had with the Columbian Fathers in Manila. He learned plenty from the Fathers about political corruption in the islands but also came to believe that the interests of the local people were being ill-served by the Peace Corps: the Filipinos wanted help with agricultural production, and "all we were sending them were teachers." Furthermore, he discovered that in at least one case a local administrator had fired a couple of his Filipino teachers, knowing that the salaries and benefits of their Peace Corps volunteer replacements would be paid by the United States government.

Bill's job became even more burdensome when another Peace Corps director left his position and Bill was given responsibility for the volunteers who had been left rudderless. The 155 volunteers who were now placed under his supervision, Bill believed, were too few to solve the locals'

On a boating excursion in the Philippines, Bill, Sarah Lee, the children, and some local friends, late 1960s. Courtesy of Chandler Marburg

needs and too many to be properly supervised in such a large country. Furthermore, he encountered difficulty in working with the secretary in Zamboanga, whom he described as "hateful." He claims that she stirred up trouble with the volunteers, comparing Bill unfavorably to the previous boss with whom she had been in love. This problem soon disappeared, though, when the woman resigned from her position. Despite Bill's misgivings about his job, Sarah Lee and the children found the new area attractive and pleasant, and she found work arranging meetings and conferences. Bill, on the other hand, unhappy with his administrative responsibilities and lacking the creative outlet that music had always provided, was ready to leave after two years. The Peace Corps director, Arthur Purcell, however, would not pay Bill's and the family's airfare home before his assignment was completed, so he hung on for the third year.

Socially, Bill and Sarah sometimes found respite in visits made by musical friends or by occasional trips to Manila and Japan. His reliable friend, Mike Seeger, made a ten-day visit, and they did some informal playing and at least one public performance. On one occasion they presented a show at a small island community that consisted of houseboats and homes that were built out into the water on stilts. Bill and Mike paddled around the island for a short time, and later picked and sang a few songs with guitar

Sarah Lee, with (left to right) Cameron, Rush, Chandler, and Grainger. Philippines, November 1969. Courtesy of Chandler Marburg

and mandolin, adding a bit of yodeling for novelty. After they finished, a local musician, who was described as a wedding singer, performed his own song and received a loud chorus of laughter and applause. When Bill and Mike asked what the singer had sung, they learned that it had been a ballad that poked fun at what was perceived as the grotesque and comical manner in which they had paddled their boat.

Bill and Sarah Lee, of course, did have opportunities to hear and see visiting entertainers or public officials. For example, in Manila they heard and visited with the American folk singer Jimmie Driftwood (James Morris), who in 1958 had become famous for his song "The Battle of New Orleans." Attendance at social functions or formal public events sponsored by the State Department and other American agencies was mandatory. On one such occasion in Manila, they attended a dinner held in honor of ambassador Mennen "Soapy" Williams and his wife. The ambassador introduced Bill to a "general" whose name was not clearly understood because of the loud music. When the general entered Bill's plane the next day, Bill learned that he was Charles Lindbergh.

Bill's tenure in the Philippines finally came to an end in 1970, and the family returned to England, but not before stopping off in late March in Claudelands, Hamilton County, New Zealand, for the National Banjo Pickers Festival.[25] The festival was in its third year, and Bill had been made aware of it by Mike Seeger, who had played there to great acclaim in 1969. Bill sang solo, performed with the Hamilton County Bluegrass Band,[26] and conducted an autoharp workshop. Interest in country music in New Zealand dated back to the 1920s, when reissues of American hillbilly records became available. Jimmie Rodgers was particularly popular there, as he was in Australia. Indigenous rural music also flourished, through the efforts of people like Slim Dusty (David Gordon Kilpatrick) and yodeling Tex Morton (Robert Lane), who moved frequently to and from Australia. Garth Gibson published a magazine called *Country and Western Spotlight* that was widely circulated among collectors and fans in both New Zealand and the United States. The bluegrass music community itself, small but ardent, was more recent and was inspired largely by the music of a group called the Hamilton County Bluegrass Band. Composed of several university-educated musicians—Alan Rhodes, Paul Trenwith, Dave Calder, Colleen Bain, Len Cohen, and Sandy McMillin—the group emerged as a festival band in 1967 and were a seasoned and well-recorded professional organization by the time they met Bill Clifton.

Although Bill Clifton's music was already well known among local bluegrass fans, his association with Mike Seeger provided an additional endorsement of his importance. After the festival of 1970 ended, Bill participated in a recording session with the Hamilton County Bluegrass Band in Auckland over the Easter weekend. He thought that he was merely making a joint appearance at the session but found out when he arrived at the studio that he was expected to perform all of the songs with the backing of the Hamilton County Band. Despite his three-year absence from music, Bill sang with strength, conviction, and competence, and his guitar and autoharp playing were exceptional. He apparently had lost nothing in his sabbatical from music, and to his surprise, his accompanying musicians knew all of his songs, or were able to learn them quickly. They had previously recorded three albums and had won considerable exposure on the television series "Country Touch," hosted by Tex Morton.

Released on the Kiwi label in 1970 as *Two Shades of Bluegrass* (SLC 93) and reissued in 2013 by the British Archive of Country Music (BACM 418), Bill's New Zealand performances remind us again of the marvelous eclecticism of his repertory. While the twenty-eight released songs did include at least two of his reliable standbys, "Mary Dear" and "Little White Washed Chimney," Bill also performed "Green to Grey," a song written by British folk revivalist Dave Goulder. The other items, though, were bedrock American country songs, including a couple of talking blues, five instrumentals featuring autoharp or guitar, and a variety of songs that came from the performances of Ernest Tubb, Uncle Dave Macon, Roy Acuff, Tex Ritter, Grandpa Jones, Carson Robison, the Carter Family, and other country stalwarts. Bill in fact reached far back to the very beginnings of commercial country music with songs borrowed from Fiddling John Carson and Ernest Stoneman, two pioneer entertainers from the twenties.

These recordings were reassuring experiences for Bill. For one thing, they reminded him that his songs were popular with bluegrass musicians around the world. They also helped him to overcome the frustrations of his experience in the Philippines, and they reminded him of how exhilarating an escape to the old songs could be. On the way home, he and the family made some side excursions, stopping in India to see the Taj Mahal, and then to the Mideast, with brief stops in Istanbul and Beirut. With every expectation that his English audience would be available to him, Bill was ready to resume his musical career.

4

A RENEWED COMMITMENT
TO FULL-TIME MUSIC, 1970 AND AFTER

Bill must have breathed a sigh of relief on his return to England in April 1970. The sojourn in the Philippines had been more frustrating than satisfying. The Peace Corps experience had been disillusioning, and his marriage had begun to disintegrate. Possibly wishing to replicate some of the cherished experiences of his rural Maryland boyhood, Bill tried to buy a small dairy farm in southeast England, complete with cows and fifty surrounding acres, but his check for a down payment bounced—a victim of a questionable decision to deposit about $16,000 of his Peace Corps earnings in a fly-by-night bank on the Channel Isle of Guernsey. A search for the bank's owner, and an effort to receive his lost deposit, proved fruitless.[1] This time Bill refused to ask his father for support. He instead rented a house in Horsted Keynes, Sussex, declaring that he had "always been a rambler" and really had no desire to be a homeowner. Sarah Lee, on the other hand, preferred to own a home, a major bone of contention between them.

Bill presumed that he could resume his musical career immediately, but he soon discovered that the English folk music scene had changed dramatically in the years he had been away. He now found that many clubs followed the policy announced by a club proprietor in Cornwall, who told him, "We are English clubs. We don't employ Americans." Singer Ewan MacColl (born Jimmie Miller) was a particularly strident exponent of this style of British musical nationalism. He railed against the spectacle of young British folk singers rambling about trying to look or sing like

Back home in England, after the Philippines experiment. Right to left: Bill, Sarah Lee, Tad, Streett, Lee Lee, Chandler, Cameron, Grainger, Rush, and the family dog, Pierceson. Horsted Keynes, England, about 1970. Courtesy of Chandler Marburg

Woody Guthrie or Bob Dylan. The husband of Peggy Seeger, MacColl insisted that singers should only sing about their home area and traditions. Although the opinionated MacColl was a controversial personality, his views carried considerable weight in the British folk music community.[2] He and Albert Lancaster (A. L.) Lloyd[3] are generally credited with being the prime generators of the British folk music revival.

Whatever the cause, Bill encountered trouble getting radio and television dates, and the radio show that he had once hosted, *Cellar Full of Folk*, had taken on a new host, Wally Whyton, and a new name, *Country Meets Folk*. "Folk music," always an amorphous term, had become even less precise in both Britain and the United States, and it increasingly encompassed virtually any performer who chose to adopt the label. Some clubs insisted on a traditional repertory of presumed indigenous material, while others, paralleling a trend found in the United States, were more receptive to singer-songwriters. Bob Dylan's influence could be felt everywhere.

Still other clubs were politically ideological—mostly left wing—and were driven by such issues as the campaign for nuclear disarmament.[4] Bill may not have been sufficiently aware of the radical/left wing nature of the British folk song community. Many of the clubs were, and always had been, political. Bill, if anything, was apolitical—liberal, but unaffiliated with any political group. After his four-year absence he now felt that the folk community was cold to him and that his involvement with the Peace Corps had made people suspicious of his political intentions, some even believing that he might be secretly complicit with the Central Intelligence Agency (CIA). This idea was reflective of a widespread view in Vietnam War–conscious England that the CIA and Peace Corps were linked.[5] The folk singer Bob Davenport, who had been godfather to one of Bill's sons, Grainger, for instance, said to Bill with incredulity, "Oh, you have diplomatic passports!" While Bill took the comment as accusatory, he had actually harbored his own suspicions that the Peace Corps had sometimes been used for covert political purposes. For example, while on a visit to the U.S. embassy in Manila in 1968, someone who was described by Bill as a CIA functionary asked him to direct Peace Corps personnel to seek some "sensitive" information from a few Muslim tribesmen (Hadji) in Zamboanga about presumed subversive activities. To some English observers Bill had been a bit suspect because he always seemed to have plenty of money, lived in big houses, had a large family, and practiced a lifestyle, including frequent vacations on the Continent, that seemed more affluent than a "folk singer" should have. And he only played small clubs! Apparently, these critics were unaware of Bill's comfortable American background.

With the avenues of commercial exposure in England becoming closed to him, Bill turned increasingly toward the performance of music on the Continent and in other parts of the world. For example, his old friend Alex Guest, who had moved to South Africa to be near his son, a professional football player, arranged a few shows and some television work for Bill in September 1973 in British East Africa. The tour was far from satisfactory, however. During a train trip from Malawi to Mozambique, Bill was prohibited from crossing the border, and the British Embassy could offer no help. He did manage to catch a flight to Salisbury, Rhodesia (now Harare, Zimbabwe), where he managed to do a couple of shows and some television work. He was bemused by the fact that the daughter of the white supremacist Ian Smith, prime minister of Rhodesia from 1964 to 1979, was the ticket taker at one of the folk clubs where he played.

Bill's reception on the European continent proved to be much more satisfactory. Prior to his stint in the Peace Corps, Bill had made a number of crucial contacts in Holland, Denmark, and Germany. He had in fact begun making extensive trips to the Continent as early as the summer of 1964, often merely for vacation, but also for occasional shows. Bill had long been interested in the Low Countries, knowing that his paternal grandfather, Charles Marburg, had been American ambassador to Belgium, and that an aunt, Christine Marburg, his father's sister, had been married to Tjarda van Starkenborgh Stachouwer, the last governor-general of the Dutch East Indies (now Indonesia). His aunt and her husband had spent the years of World War II in a Japanese war camp.[6]

Bill did extensive television work in Holland, and he received considerable exposure in the Dutch press. Much of his activity there was promoted by CMS Productions, a booking agency owned and operated by a Dutch couple, Cor and Margaret Sanne, who had heard Bill in concert in late 1971. Bill, in turn, introduced them to other bluegrass musicians such as Bill Monroe and Mac Wiseman. The Sannes went on to found one of Europe's leading music journals, *Country Gazette*, while also working as promoters of such well-known American country entertainers as Don Williams and George Hamilton IV.[7]

Bill Clifton with the Big Bear, Richard Weize (1970s). Courtesy of Richard Weize

Bill's European involvement received additional support in 1970 when he met Richard Weize.[8] Born in Germany on August 4, 1945, Weize had prospered as a wine merchant for a French company, Pieroth, one of the largest wine companies in Europe. He had also loved and collected American popular music since he was a child, when he first heard and bought Bill Haley's "Rock around the Clock." He concentrated on rock and roll until a friend gave him a country LP that included selections by the superstars Don Gibson and Jim Reeves. At $3.98 each, the American LPs he found seemed to be too great a bargain for a budding young collector to resist. The wine business often took Weize to England, where he lived from 1965 to 1971. At the International Festival of Country Music, held at the Wembley Stadium in 1969, he met the American singers George Hamilton IV, Skeeter Davis (Mary Frances Penick), and Bill Clifton. By 1971 Weize had returned to Germany and had launched into the music business full time, recording mostly American acts, country and popular, and booking talent in various parts of the Continent.

Weize experimented with several recording ventures, including the Folk-Variety label, with his first project being a renewed offering of the music of the pioneer American cowboy singer Carl Sprague.[9] In 1975 Weize produced an LP of the unissued recordings that Bill and Paul Clayton had made back in 1952 at the University of Virginia, hoping vainly that New York's Stinson label would issue them. After seeing an engraving of a family of bears in an 1898 encyclopedia, Weize inaugurated the Bear Family label, marked by a logo picturing a bear and four cubs. The first Bear Family release was Bill Clifton's two-LP set, *Going Back to Dixie.* Bill was thinking of Weize when he recorded an American children's song, "Waltzing with Bears," for a twenty-year anniversary collection for Bear Family, and, in a good-natured spoof of Weize, changed the name of the song's protagonist from Uncle Walter to Uncle Richard.[10]

Weize concentrated primarily on the reissuance of recordings, building an enormous catalog of albums that became famous worldwide for their state-of-the-art production and historical analysis. Each Bear box collection included an accompanying book of recording data, artist biographies, historical narrative, and photographs. Influenced by his mother, who was a schoolteacher, Weize emphasized the historical context of each album/artist and insisted on accurate details. In his early business dealings, however, Weize ruffled a lot of feathers with his brusque aggressiveness and his casual use of recorded material, that is, his failure to obtain permission or to provide adequate compensation. For instance, when the old-time singer and banjo player Grandpa Jones found some of his material being used without permission, he brought legal action against Weize and secured a cease-and-desist order and at least a partial compensation for the material that had been sold. Ultimately, though, Bear Family did issue a fine five-disc compilation of Jones's recordings called *Everybody's Grandpa*.

Although Bill has had his own differences with Weize through the years, their relationship proved to be mutually beneficial. Bill introduced Weize to several old-time American musicians, such as Jim Eanes and Mac Odell, and supplied him with reams of information about country and bluegrass music. Weize, on the other hand, promoted many of Bill's shows and contributed greatly to the documentation of Bill's earlier recorded output through his monumental ten-CD box collection of Bill's music—*Around the World to Poor Valley*, issued on the Bear label (BCD 16425 HK) on June 6, 2001.

More immediately, Weize began arranging radio and television work for Bill, while booking him frequently in Hamburg, Berlin, and other German cities. One 1971 concert in Berlin attracted more than ten thousand people. On August 30, 1975, Bill was reunited with his old friends, the Echo Mountain Boys, for a popular television series called *Der Musikladen* (The Music Shop), carried on Radio Bremen.[11] Although the show was basically rock and pop oriented, on this occasion the music was country themed, and Bill shared the stage with a local country group and pop singer Alexis Korner, who did a mixed set of rock, blues, and folk tunes. Bill and the boys were permitted to do several country numbers, including a couple of vintage gospel songs, "Turn Your Radio On" and "I Saw the Light." In the performance of "I Saw the Light," which can be seen and heard on YouTube, Bill was joined by Korner, who shouts his way through the choruses. The effect seems decidedly less spiritual than Bill might have wanted.

Although most of Bill's performances were apparently solo affairs, Weize sometimes booked him with other entertainers, such as Hedy West, with whom Bill had performed and recorded in both the United States and England.[12] Bill had played with Hedy in July 1965 at the Cambridge Festival, but his first recording venture with her had apparently come in 1967 when he returned to the United States to prepare for his mission in the Philippines. Bill, Hedy, and Mike Seeger recorded seventeen songs in three August sessions at the Edgewood Studio in Washington, D.C. Bill was pleased to find active work on the European continent after 1970, but he did not particularly enjoy playing in the German clubs. On one occasion, Bill and Red Rector arrived for a long-scheduled show and found that it had been preempted by a rock concert. He and Red received their promised fee, however, prompting Red to say that it was the first time he had ever been paid for *not* doing a show. On another occasion at a club in Hamburg, when Bill was performing with Hedy, the duo found the scene distasteful because the smoking was "intense." When she expressed her displeasure with the smokers in the audience, the club owner angrily announced that the customers were free to smoke.

Hedwig Grace "Hedy" West was born on April 6, 1938, in Cartersville, Georgia, the daughter of the poet and labor activist Don West. She inherited her father's passion for racial and social justice, and her family's love for traditional balladry—her paternal grandmother, Lillie Mulkey West, was a singer and banjo player. While studying drama at Columbia University, Hedy became active in the Greenwich Village folk scene, caught the attention of Pete Seeger, and made a few albums for New York's Vanguard label. Along with her performance of older material, she also wrote or revised a number of songs and saw her arrangement of "500 Miles" become one of the most popular songs in the folk revival, with country singer Bobby Bare's recorded performance probably the most widely known version.[13]

By the mid-1960s Hedy had moved to England and was making frequent forays to Germany, where she strived to perform in both German and English. In England she appeared at the Keele and Cambridge Folk Festivals in 1965 and sang frequently with Bill at clubs in England and Scotland. While musical collaboration consumed much of their time, Bill later insisted that their relationship was strictly platonic. Nevertheless, Hedy could still remember Bill with much fondness many years later. In a discussion on the Mudcat Café site in 2000, where Bill's recent vacation on an undisclosed tropical island was mentioned, Hedy responded, "I can imagine Bill luxuriating in the velvet of the tropics. He plays velvet, sings velvet, talks velvet, too."[14]

As early as August 1967, Hedy, Bill, and Mike Seeger recorded a variety of songs, mostly old-time country, at the Edgewood Studios in Washington, D.C. In August 1972 Bill and Hedy, along with the highly regarded mandolinist Andrew Townend, recorded eight songs at the International Studio in London. Later that year Hedy and Bill collaborated on an LP for Weize's Folk-Variety label, *Getting Folk Out of the Country* (recorded in London and released in 1974). The album eventually appeared on the

Bear label as both an LP and a CD. Bill claimed that it was really Hedy's album, but while she did play the most prominent role as lead vocalist and five-string banjoist, Bill made distinctive contributions as an instrumentalist and singer. He sang solo on "Mary of the Wild Moor" and "Whitehouse Blues," sang harmony on most of the other numbers, and provided instrumental backup on the guitar and autoharp. Sarah Lee and two Marburg daughters, Chandler and Cameron (Camie), lent a choral effect to one song, "Angel Band," by providing harmony on the choruses. The album as a whole may not have been quite as important as Weize claimed it to be—he called it a "memorable meeting of two legends," a collaboration between a working-class musician and an upper-class musician—but it was a generally successful performance. It has generated considerable positive discussion over the years in such folk music websites as The Mudcat Café.

By this time in his life Bill had once again made a full commitment to music but had become increasingly estranged from Sarah Lee. The reasons for the estrangement are not entirely clear; they after all had shared ten years of marriage and had raised seven children. Bill will only say that the marriage had been wrong from the beginning and that he had been pressured into the relationship (by whom, he does not say). That they were moving in different directions had become obvious during the Philippines interlude, but the rift widened considerably as Bill's heightened performance schedule kept him on the road and away from home. Absorbed in his musical pursuits, he seems to have been a rather poor communicator and too often neglected to contact his wife and family for long periods. Bill frankly did not like to be bothered with personal problems while he was on tour, and he even discouraged Sarah Lee from trying to reach him by phone. Bill clearly preferred the company of his musician friends. When he returned from tours, he was tired and wanted to rest, or was ready to prepare for his next trip and to relearn old song material. One cannot be certain whether other women were involved in Bill's life, but as an attractive man and charismatic entertainer, the temptations were always available.

It is difficult to pinpoint precisely the date and cause of their marital collapse, but a venture known as the Hoathly Hill Experiment seems to have brought matters to a head.[15] Bill, as we have seen, resisted home ownership, probably fearing further financial obligations to his father, while Sarah Lee longed for the stability of a home that she could call her own. While in the Philippines, she and Bill had become interested in the theories of Rudolf Steiner, an Austrian educator and philosopher who promoted a wide range of ideas, including biodynamic agriculture and Waldorf education (so named because of a lecture Steiner gave to workers in 1919 at the Waldorf-Astoria cigarette factory in Stuttgart). Steiner promoted a multisensory and holistic approach to education designed to involve the child in creative play, develop artistic expression and social capacities, and encourage critical and empathetic understanding through math, the arts and sciences, the humanities, and world languages.[16]

When the Marburgs returned to England, Sarah Lee met Christian Thal-Jantzen and his wife, and three other couples who were also deeply invested in the philosophy and educational ideas of Rudolf Steiner. In 1972 Sarah Lee insisted that the Marburg family join a communal project called Hoathly Hill, near Horsted Keynes in West Sussex. Their new residence was a twelve-bedroom Victorian gabled house, with outbuildings, surrounded by twenty-six acres, governed by another Steiner commitment: sustainable agriculture. Chartered as a housing association, with some of the properties rented out, the experiment required living in a common space with shared communal responsibilities. One observer called it "a blend of sixties radicalism and seventies optimism." Bill reluctantly agreed to commit $10,000 to the project but did so only after securing a loan from a Baltimore bank, a decision that once again placed him under an unwanted obligation to his father, who had assumed responsibility for the debt. While he had consented to the financial payment, Bill never liked the living arrangements at Hoathly Hill. Fifteen people, for example, shared the kitchen, and Bill, who assumed the task of buying groceries for everyone, felt that the other participants did not pay their fair share toward the day-to-day living expenses. Within a year, he and Sarah Lee had both become disaffected with communal living, and they moved into a rented home—called Yggdrasil—across from Michael Hall, the Rudolf Steiner Waldorf School, where the children were enrolled. Sarah Lee had become deeply immersed in Waldorf education and soon began spending time in Germany studying to become an art therapist. With Bill gone on music tours for lengthy periods, the kids were too often left under the care of babysitters. To further complicate matters, Bill and Sarah Lee had also begun relationships with other people, and their separation was soon complete.

Well before the collapse of the Hoathly Hill venture, Bill had embarked on an important new direction in musical performance that entailed increased travel back to the United States. While he had made occasional trips to America to visit his parents or for recording purposes, he did not publicly perform there again until 1972. On June 3 he and John Atkins, a British accountant and folk club proprietor, traveled to the Indian Springs Festival held at the KOA campground near Hagerstown, Maryland, an event sponsored by *Bluegrass Unlimited* magazine. Followed by appearances on successive weekends that summer at Ralph Stanley's festival, near his old home place in McClure, Virginia, and at Bean Blossom in Indiana, the event marked the beginning of one of the most artistically exciting and satisfying phases of Bill's career.

The Indian Springs festival was primarily the brainchild of Pete Kuyken-dall and was designed in part to counter the unsavory reputation that some of the bluegrass and rock festivals had gained in the late sixties and early seventies. Like many in the bluegrass field, Kuykendall had been appalled by the rampant hedonism exhibited by some of the youth who attended the festivals, particularly the huge affair in Union Grove, North Carolina, that had become notorious for the blatant presence there of dope and alcohol. The Indian Springs Festival quickly earned the reputation of being a well-organized, drug-free, and music-driven scene. Bill Clifton could not have chosen a more appropriate venue to showcase his tradition-based style of bluegrass music or to reinvigorate his American career. The Indian Springs Festival also came in the context of a resurgence nationally of the bluegrass style. Although Mike Seeger played with him at the festival, Bill did not have his own band. He was fortunate, however, to receive the backing of some of the musicians who were in the forefront of this revitalization. He was reunited with John Duffey, Tom Gray, and their new band, Seldom Scene, who were also making their first appearance at the festival.

Organized in 1971 through a series of Tuesday-night jam sessions held in banjo-player Ben Eldridge's basement in Bethesda, Maryland, Seldom Scene became one of the most popular bands in the bluegrass field while being one of the least active. Although their intent was to "keep their day jobs" and maintain a low profile of weekly shows with little active touring, Seldom Scene became famous for their progressive repertory, smooth vocal harmonies, and stellar musicianship. Like the Country Gentlemen earlier in his career, the Seldom Scene were in many ways dramatically different from Bill Clifton, but they adapted easily to his songs and style.

The Indian Springs Festival not only launched Bill's renewed American career, it also brought him in contact with Red Rector.[17] One night, while walking through the festival grounds at Indian Springs, Bill heard William Eugene "Red" Rector playing his mandolin in a jam session with Don

Red Rector and Bill Clifton (early 1970s). Courtesy of Bill Clifton

Reno. Bill joined in with his guitar and found that he and Red sounded good together and enjoyed performing the same kind of songs. He asked Red if he would like to go overseas and, receiving an affirmative response, helped him obtain a passport only a few days after the festival. Bill had never known Rector personally but was aware of the recent and superb LP that he had made with Fred Smith in 1969 for the County label—*Songs From the Heart of the Country* (County 721), a collection of beautifully performed vintage country duets. Bill of course had long been impressed by Red's musical past, a career that included stints with Carl Story, Charlie Monroe, Frank "Hylo" Brown, and other bluegrass stalwarts, and he probably knew that Red's contributions as a "sideman" were not always adequately acknowledged or appreciated. Bill had already come to believe that the supercharged bluegrass field needed a respite from the hard-driving banjo sound, as well as a revitalization of good old-fashioned duet singing, and he felt that he and Red could satisfy those goals.

Red was born on December 15, 1929, in the little town of Marshall in Madison County, North Carolina—a citadel of traditional country music—and was given a good Southern name, Billy Gene. He was unaware that this name was on his birth certificate until he applied for a passport. William

Eugene, his preferred moniker, began dabbling with the mandolin when he was a small child. In 1944 the precocious teenager played with J. E. and Wade Mainer on a radio show called *The Old Chisholm Trail*, produced in New York by Alan Lomax for CBS and the BBC. Red was in good company for this broadcast, playing with the likes of Woody Guthrie, Burl Ives, Cisco Houston, and Lily May Ledford (of the Coon Creek Girls).

While Red had a strong baritone voice and was adept at both lead and harmony singing, he was most famous for his mandolin style. Like many mandolin players in bluegrass and old-time music, Red had been initially influenced by the playing of Bill Monroe, but he was also attracted to the jazz-inflected styles of people like Kenneth "Jethro" Burns and Paul Buskirk. Red could compete favorably with any "progressive" musician, but at heart he remained wedded to old-time music, particularly to the soulful and close harmony sounds and songs of such brother duets as Charlie and Bill Monroe and Bill and Earl Bolick (the Blue Sky Boys). His instrumental style was fluid and inventive but melody based, qualities that appealed to Bill Clifton.

Bill had initially thought that the team of Fred and Red might be talked into making a European tour. Fred Smith, though, refused to take a plane trip, and, in any case, Red believed that Fred's corny Southern humor would never be accepted by European audiences. Red consequently went to Europe on his own in 1974, and then as part of a duo with Bill in the years that followed. Red and Bill recorded for a variety of labels in both Europe and the United States, but their most productive and influential recordings were made for the American-based County label. County's initial association with Bill Clifton had begun with an LP of material originally recorded by Bill in the late fifties, but in June 1974, Bill went back into the studio for a collection of new recordings, *Come By the Hills* (County 751). Bill was joined by an all-star lineup consisting of Red, John Duffey, Walt Hensley, Tom Gray, Mike Seeger, and Kenny Baker (the Kentucky musician whom Bill Monroe described as "the best fiddler in bluegrass music"). Although Bill recorded mostly older American songs, such as "Pretty Flowers" and "Blue Eyed Elaine," the title cut, "Come By the Hills," was a lilting song written by the Scottish journalist and playwright W. Gordon Smith. Set to a traditional Irish tune, the song became a special favorite for Red.

The affiliation with the County label provided Bill a record company that was not only compatible with his old-time orientation but one that was also in the vanguard of the string band revival of the seventies. The label was owned by David Freeman, a former railroad postal worker and transplanted New Yorker, who was now living in Floyd, Virginia. As a teenager, Freeman had become fascinated with hillbilly music and with Southern rural culture. His ardent affection for the rural South equaled that held by Bill Clifton. One of a number of factors that contributed to Freeman's love for the music was a trip he and his family made in 1953 down U.S. Route 11 through the South to New Orleans. He recalled that country radio shows provided the soundtrack for the entire trip. Freeman received further indoctrination to country music from the records played by a very popular and influential disk jockey in the Northeast, Don Larkin, on his *Hometown Frolic* broadcast on WAAT in Newark, New Jersey, or from concerts promoted by Larkin (sometimes described as Barkin' Larkin) at the Terrace Ballroom in Newark. Freeman had seen Bill Clifton there in 1956 or 1957.[18]

Freeman converted his passion for old hillbilly 78 rpm records into a company that initially specialized in reissues drawn from Freeman's personal collection. Still living in New York in 1964, Freeman had produced his first County LP, *A Collection of Mountain Fiddle Music* (County 501), an anthology of songs taken from old 78 rpm hillbilly records, and by 1965 had established a mail-order business called County Sales. By 1974 he was distributing bluegrass and old-time recordings around the world, and he had relocated his operations to the little Blue Ridge Mountain village of Floyd, Virginia. Freeman had also moved beyond the exclusive reissuance of old records. Drawing on the research and field recordings made by the New Jersey musician and collector Charles Faurot,[19] County began issuing the recordings of still-living old-time performers, mostly clawhammer banjo players and fiddlers from Virginia and North Carolina. One of them, Tommy Jarrell, from Toast, North Carolina, who was both a fiddler and banjo player, became the godfather of the modern string band revival. Fledgling string musicians from all over the country made pilgrimages to Tommy's home, prospering from his hospitality, wit, and patient instruction.

The County recordings introduced Bill's name and music to a new generation of bluegrass and country fans. He and Red recorded for County again on July 15–16, 1975, *Another Happy Day* (County 758) and on September 13–15, 1976, *Clifton and Company* (County 765). The latter item was issued as a Bill Clifton record, but both LPs highlighted the duet sound of the two men. With their emphasis on rare or under-recorded older songs, they won acclaim for their musicianship and historical documentation. In the meantime, Bill and Red had continued to record for the German Bear label and had embarked on a series of tours in the United States, Europe, and, ultimately, Japan.

Their first extended tour, booked by Richard Weize, was a six-week engagement in 1975 through Denmark, Holland, and Germany. During this tour they recorded an album for Weize in northern Germany, *Are You from Dixie?*, on which they were joined by a Swiss musician, Jean-Blaise Rochat. Born on September 14, 1946, in Lausanne, Switzerland, and trained as a urologist, Rochat had been introduced to Bill's music through the Starday LP, *Mountain Folk Songs*, a compilation that converted many to Bill's music throughout the world. Rochat also joined Bill on European tours in 1976 and 1978 and has remained a friend and musical companion ever since, typically performing with Bill's group, the Pick of the Crop, or with his own aggregation, JB's Band, which included some of the same musicians.

Bill's active involvement in the European musical scene came in the context of a worldwide embrace of the bluegrass idiom by many young musicians like Rochat. Bill was not the exclusive catalyst in every case, but bluegrass musicians everywhere profited from the music he had made and from his active encouragement. Practical evidence of the internationalization of bluegrass came in 1971 when a band from New Zealand—the Hamilton County Band, and a band from Japan—Bluegrass 45, appeared to very positive reviews at Bean Blossom (Bill Monroe's festival in Indiana) and other festivals in the United States and on the stage of the *Grand Ole Opry*. Bill Clifton had lent support to both groups, as well as to others during his time abroad. He was now thrilled to see a continuing stream of musicians emerging who shared his love for American old-time and bluegrass music. Charles Newman of Lowestoft, Suffolk, England, and Rodney McElrea of Omagh, County Tyrone, in Northern Ireland, played major roles in the distribution of American country LPs in Europe through their magazine, *Country News and Views*. Dave Freeman, of County Sales, said, "As a matter of fact, that is really how we got started into the business full time," by supplying records and CDs to the customers the British magazine had drummed up.

Another young European enthusiast who promoted both Bill's career and the larger cause of European bluegrass expansion was a Dutchman named Rienk Janssen. Janssen had originally come to country music through an interest in the country-and-western superstar, Jim Reeves (a singer who was

Rienk Janssen: the benefactor of bluegrass in Europe (2014). Courtesy of Rienk Janssen

widely popular in Europe and even South Africa). Janssen's discovery of Bill Clifton's music came as an accident, a byproduct of his record-collecting habits. Janssen is quick to say that he discovered the music of Bill Clifton because an LP he found—*The Bluegrass Sound of Bill Clifton*—sold for only $1.69! Once the bluegrass bug bit him, Janssen became a tireless collector of the music, and an energetic promoter of the style throughout Europe. His promotional magazine, *Strictly Country*, endured for forty years, from 1971 to 2011, and evolved into a very active engine of music promotion. In 1982 he and a few associates had organized one of the most successful bluegrass festivals in Europe at Zuidlaren in the Netherlands. Janssen's relationship with Bill Clifton has been long and faithful, and when Bill's stupendous Bear Family collection, *Around the World to Poor Valley*, appeared in 2001, Janssen wrote the accompanying biographical notes.[20]

The last years of Bill's European involvement, and the first of his renewed American career, also came in association with Red Rector. Bill and Red worked together every summer from 1976 until Red's death in 1990. Red did their American booking, and Bill did the scheduling in Europe. While musicianship was obviously Red's premiere contribution to the act, his stage personality—marked by an affable, easygoing nature, and quick wit and humor—was also a winning attribute. As a musician, though, with his seemingly effortless mandolin riffs and uncanny gifts for improvisation, Red was unsurpassed. Mandolin players everywhere labored to find out how such a shower of notes, syncopated but still somehow melodic, could be produced on such a small instrument. The evidence for this virtuosity remains documented in the recordings that Red made over a long professional career, in a few YouTube videos, and particularly in the recordings made with Bill at a live performance in Coventry, England, on March 22, 1976. Red and Bill had performed earlier that month in Schellerton, Germany, and had then crossed the Channel to England by ferry; they immediately drove to Coventry, where they arrived dog-tired to play a show. Despite his apparent exhaustion, Red gave one of the greatest performances of his life. Preserved on a reel-to-reel tape recorder, much of the material was eventually released in 2003 on a CD bearing the imprimatur of Bill's own Elf recording label. It was called *Alive!* (Elf 104), and it captured the two musicians at the height of their musical powers.

Although Bill performed tirelessly during these years, he continued his campaign to publicize American old-time musicians in Europe. The highlight of this effort came when Bill Monroe and the Blue Grass Boys came to England in April 1975. Bill had been involved in Monroe's first English tour in 1966, but on this second series of shows he played a more central organizing role, arranging the dates with his old friend John Atkins. Bill also sang occasionally during this event and even enjoyed the privilege of joining Monroe on a few duets, such as the Monroe standards "Sweetheart, You Done Me Wrong" and "Little Cabin Home on the Hill." In his recollections of the tour, Bob Black—Monroe's five-string banjo player—gave Bill Clifton much credit for the tour's success, saying that his "knowledge and experience of performing in Britain and Europe made him very good at showing us around and making us feel comfortable."

Monroe appeared in Wembley and other sites in England, but his visit to Scotland was the one that delighted him most. Proud of his Scottish heritage, he sometimes spoke of "the ancient tones" that supposedly underlay his music. On April 25 Monroe and the Blue Grass Boys played at the Greyfriars Monastery in Uddingston, Scotland, an ancient dwelling marked by stone walls, wooden floors, and a roaring log fire. Fittingly, Monroe began his concert with "I'm on My Way Back to the Old Home." Reviewer Jim Hyndman, a Scottish musician and country music club proprietor, called the concert "the single most important event in Scottish bluegrass history . . . the night Bill Monroe came home."[21]

While England and the Continent continued to be fertile grounds of performance for Bill Clifton, he played an important role also as ambassador for bluegrass music in Japan. In 1976 he and Red appeared in Japan with a trio of musicians appropriately described for the event as the Bluegrass All-Stars: Bill Keith, Jim Brock, and Tom Gray. Bill had performed earlier in Japan, first in the summer of 1967 during an impromptu side excursion while on his way to the Philippines to take up his job with the Peace Corps, and then again in the fall of 1968 during a brief vacation. On these trips, Bill was introduced to the enthusiastic passion of Japanese bluegrass fans, was wined and dined and treated like royalty. In his 1967 concert he was backed by a local band of Japanese musicians who called themselves the Dixie Mountain Boys.

Japanese interest in bluegrass and other forms of country music began during American military occupation right after World War II. The real upsurge of interest, though, came through the music of Lester Flatt and Earl Scruggs, who were well known in Japanese bluegrass circles because of their recordings and their appearance in the soundtrack of the popular Beverley Hillbillies television show. They also visited the country in March 1968. Japanese bluegrass aficionados knew about Bill Clifton because of the indefatigable promotions of Don Pierce, who gave tapes of Bill's music to visiting Japanese musicians and encouraged the reissuance of his records in Japan. Pierce visited that country for about a month in early 1965 and later told *Billboard* magazine that he had found "a tremendous upsurge" of interest and sales for country music in Japan. Working with Michio Matsuede, who directed Starday's office in Japan, and with promoter and musician Masaaki Inagaki, Pierce spent much time touting Bill Clifton's records, particularly those on the London label. Inagaki especially loved Bill's recording of "When You Kneel at Mother's Grave," an affection apparently shared by several other Japanese bluegrass musicians, some of whom can still be seen and heard performing the song on YouTube.

Bill received prominent support from a couple of pioneering Japanese bluegrass musicians, half-brothers Toshio Watanabe and Sab "Watanabe" Inoue, who had worked tirelessly to generate support for bluegrass in Japan. They had performed since the mid-1960s in a band called Bluegrass 45 (named for the famous traditional song "Train 45" and for the year 1945, when bluegrass music had supposedly first emerged). Their first professional gigs came in the port city of Kobe at the Lost City coffeehouse (named for the American old-time music band, the New Lost City Ramblers). Through the encouragement of Dick Freeland, owner of the Rebel record label in Charlottesville, Virginia, who heard them in 1970 at the Kobe coffeehouse, Bluegrass 45 came to the United States in 1971 and appeared at a large number of venues, including the Bean Blossom Festival in Indiana and the *Grand Ole Opry*. Upon their return to Japan, they embarked on a very active campaign to promote bluegrass music in that country, largely through the Takarazuka Festival (begun in 1972 and remembered by Bill as a very family-oriented event), the establishment of a monthly bluegrass magazine called *Moonshiner*, and a mail-order concern called BOM (bluegrass and old-time music) Services. Clearly modeled on David Freeman's County Sales, BOM imported American musical material and made it available to Japanese fans and musicians. Bill Clifton received constant promotional support through this outlet, as well as encouragement to play in Japan, where he played five times (with the last show coming in 2003). He found the experiences to be exhausting, however—"it's always nice to go there, but it's also very tiring"—because the Japanese were so intense in their love for the music and in their desire to be as close as possible to the musicians.[22]

As Bill's international music career heated up, so did his relationship with the newest love in his life, Tineke Labrie. Bill met Tineke in Holland in 1971. At the time she was married to a banjo player named Jerry Gout, who played with a band called the Clodhoppers and who was a fan of Bill's music. Music brought the musicians into frequent proximity, and Jerry's band sometimes supported Bill in his concerts. Bill seems to have been immediately smitten with Tineke and was occasionally flirtatious with her. When he first visited the Gouts' home, he saw their two little girls and said, "There sure are a lot of pretty girls in this house." Bill's marriage to Sarah Lee had by this time disintegrated. Although Tineke and Jerry Gout were still technically married, she and Bill were together constantly after November 1975. She accompanied Bill to America in 1976, met his family in Maryland, and went along with him to his various concerts around the country. Much of the time they lived and traveled in a Ford station wagon that was large enough to accommodate two foam mattresses. Walter Broderick, the proprietor of the Red Fox Inn in Bethesda, Maryland, where Bill, Red, and Mike Seeger played an extended engagement, obtained a work permit for Tineke. She took tickets at the door and apparently kept a close watch on people who tried to use their reputations or alleged influence to gain admission. Ralph Rinzler, for example, who was head of the Smithsonian Folklife Festival and a close friend of Mike Seeger's, tried, along with a few close friends, to enter the Red Fox Inn without paying, but he found the way blocked by Tineke.

Eventually divorced from their respective spouses, Bill and Tineke married in Holland on October 31, 1978. She brought two more children (Flory and Stella) into Bill's extended family, and they later had their own child, Laurel. Bill's older children, though, were no longer under his direct supervision, and the younger ones remained with Sarah Lee. She had fallen in love with and married Jeffrey Sexton, a fellow disciple of Rudolf Steiner. Sara Lee and Jeffrey had moved to the nonprofit, Steiner-influenced Lukas Community in Temple, New Hampshire, where Sarah Lee taught an art class for the cognitively disabled.[23]

Bill and Tineke were also ready to move back to the United States. The most immediate pressing problem with which they had to contend was the question of where they should settle down. While searching for a home of their own, they depended on the hospitality of friends, living at various times with Red Rector in Knoxville, Bill's parents in Baltimore, and with Tom Gray in Washington, D.C. It is no surprise that Bill seems to have been determined to live in the South. He and Tineke considered a few sites in East Tennessee, and Boone, North Carolina, and even in Maine, but they eventually settled on a home in Mendota in Southwest Virginia near the old Carter Family home place. Bill's romantic fixation with all things Carter Family had again affected his decision making. He and Tineke found an old, rundown house with a couple of acres and paid for it with the $25,000 Tineke obtained from her father. They also began buying furniture, and, with the assistance of one of A. P.'s nephews, Jack Carter, they embarked on the slow job of restoration. Life in Mendota was

Bill and Tineke at their Virginia Home, 1980. Courtesy of Bill Clifton

at first good for Tineke, and she seemed to enjoy the setting. She got a job with a mental health facility in nearby Bristol, working with patients in their homes.[24] But eventually the isolation of the area, and the cultural gap that she perceived between herself and her neighbors, made her long for a more comfortable situation.

In the meantime, Bill's efforts to maintain a viable full-time professional music career once again ran into a roadblock. Among other things, the necessity for alimony and child support for some of his younger children, who now lived in New Hampshire with their mother, added to his financial burden. Because of the sporadic nature and uncertainty of his musical career, particularly the difficulty of finding gigs in winter, Bill took a job with the Tenneva Food Company in Bristol, Tennessee, in the spring of 1979.

Except for milking cows as a child and, of course, the grueling hours spent in marine boot camp, working for the Tenneva Food Company was the hardest physical work Bill had ever done, and the job brought him into intimate contact with the working-class people he had sung about most of his life. He worked for the company from 1979 to 1982 and did just about every kind of labor that was required, working first in the factory, then in the office, and then out on the road as a salesman. The warehouse work was particularly arduous, requiring Bill to go in and out of the freezer, loading trucks.

The Mendota years definitely had their bleak moments, particularly during the winter months, when it was hard to heat a big rambling house that had only a woodstove and fireplace for warmth. The family, which at this time consisted of Bill, Tineke, and daughters Flory, Stella, and baby Laurel (born in 1980), actually had to subsist on food stamps for about six months. Nevertheless, a spring garden provided a welcome supply of fresh vegetables. Flory remembers these years as idyllic in many ways, enjoying the quiet rural countryside, the "smell of burning wood and the crackling sounds of the fireplace," and the joy of digging her toes in the fresh garden dirt. Laurel, on the other hand, was never enamored of Virginia rural life, and she sought escape through books and her love for animals and nature.

Bill left the Tenneva Food Company in 1982 and went to work as a salesman for a radio station in Gate City, Virginia, selling broadcast time. After about a month he had to go back to England on a business trip and found upon his return to the United States that the station had hired someone else. He then moved to an Arlington radio station for a year and a half. To make matters worse, the Baltimore bank now requested payment on the loan that had been made for the Hoathly Hill property; with interest, it now totaled $18,000. Fearing that they might lose the Mendota place, Tineke pleaded for help from Bill's parents, and Grainger Marburg immediately paid off the loan. During these unsteady times, Bill's mother did try to persuade him and Tineke to move back home to Maryland, arguing that he could work for his father and live in one of the houses on the estate. Bill, however, opted for the "independence" and distance he had always sought from his father.

Through all these difficulties, Bill had refused to put his music on hold. Tenneva, in fact, had been fairly generous in permitting him to embark on occasional music tours. Bill's musical output during these years remained at a superior level. In 1978 the great banjo player Don Stover had joined Bill and Red as the First Generation Trio. Born on March 6, 1928, in Ameagle, Raleigh County, West Virginia, Stover had worked as a coal miner but had played music since he was a child. He was a veteran musician with much professional experience. His most famous and longest-lasting stint began in 1952, when he moved to Boston and began playing six nights a week with a duo of transplanted West Virginians, the Lilly Brothers (Everett and Bea), during their lengthy stay at a seedy joint called Hillbilly Ranch. He remained with them, off and on, until 1970.

Stover brought a creditable ability as a baritone singer to the group but was most highly valued as a five-string banjoist. Bill and Red were both

Bill, Tineke, and daughters Stella, Laurel, and Flory (at Selsed, mid-1980s). Courtesy of Bill Clifton

impressed with Stover's ability to move easily from the Scruggs three-finger style to the older frailing or drop-thumb style in the midst of a song, without missing a beat. Don played his first show with Bill and Red in June 1978 at the West Virginia Arts and Crafts Festival at Harper's Ferry. At the initial West Virginia appearance Joe Wilson, the festival organizer and long-time executive director of the National Council for the Traditional Arts, paid the trio $2,000—a significant advance over the $700 they typically received. Wilson dubbed the group the First Generation, an indication of the trio's combined experience and of their presence when the bluegrass style was originally taking shape. Richard Spottswood maintained that this was "the first time bluegrass had seen a new group formed from established performers."[25]

Throughout the decade of the 1980s and beyond, Bill was finally doing what he had always longed to do; he was making music the exclusive pursuit of his life, playing most of the nation's leading festivals, usually during the spring and summer months. While he played in a wide variety of festivals in the Southeast, Pennsylvania, Florida, and the Midwest, Harper's Ferry in West Virginia was an exceptional favorite. Held in a beautiful setting at the confluence of the Shenandoah and Potomac Rivers, the Mountain Arts and Crafts Festival at Harper's Ferry welcomed Bill to its stage for more than thirty years.

When Art Stamper brought his fiddle to the band in 1990, Bill attained the presence of not only one of the greatest fiddlers in the bluegrass world, but also a link to the earliest days of the music's history. Stamper was born into a family of old-time fiddlers in Hindman County, Kentucky, on November 1, 1933, and by the time he teamed up with Bill Clifton he had played with many of the veterans of bluegrass music, such as Red Allen, the Goins Brothers, the Osborne Brothers, and the Stanley Brothers. He had been with the Stanleys when they were at their best, at the time of their historic first Mercury sessions in 1953. When he wasn't on the road fiddling, Stamper was making his living in Louisville as a hairdresser in his salon, The Way of Art.

The cherished and highly productive association with Red Rector came to an untimely end one spring afternoon—May 31, 1990—when Red suffered a heart attack while out mowing his lawn. Red had no prior history of heart trouble. Bill said, "It was one of the few times I ever cried over a death." A few days earlier they had practiced at Bill's house for a recording to be made later that year for Strictly Country Records in the Netherlands.

They drifted into a discussion of the possibility of death after practicing the venerable gospel song, "Who Will Sing for Me?" Bill and Tineke sang the song at Red's casket during graveside services. Bill also sang one of Red's favorite songs, the Irish ballad "Come By the Hills," while Art Stamper provided fiddle accompaniment. The notes to the song are carved on Red's tombstone.

Red's death delivered an emotional and psychological blow that Bill found hard to overcome. No musical association had ever been as important to him. First Generation had booked a large number of shows, including two festivals in West Virginia (Harper's Ferry and Summersville) and at the Father's Day Festival held at Grass Valley, California (the largest and oldest festival on the West Coast). Don Stover, however, did not want to make the trip to California, so Bill began thinking about stopgap and workable alternatives. He even tried to persuade old-time musician Zeke Morris (one of Bill's childhood heroes) to come out of retirement to sing with him. Zeke declined, however, feeling that if he got involved he might have to travel to Europe. Consequently, Bill did the West Virginia shows, but cancelled the rest.

Bill fought during these years to maintain control over his recordings, working hard to find labels that would enable him to record the kind of material that he favored. In the late 1980s he had learned from a late-night television ad that his early recordings on the Starday label were being sold by Gusto, a company that had not paid him any royalties. Later, in Canada at a folk festival, he found people selling the Gusto recordings of his work at a price lower than that received for those he sold at his performances. Furious, Bill obtained a lawyer and recovered damages while also receiving the return of his original Starday masters, which at the time were unlawfully in the possession of Gusto.[26] These masters later became the content of a CD, *The Early Years, 1957–1958*, released in 1992 on Rounder 1021. Containing his most beloved early recordings—including "Mary Dear," "Little White Washed Chimney," "Blue Ridge Mountain Blues," and "My Old Pal of Yesterday"—the CD contributed greatly to the revitalization of Bill's career.

With a whole summer of dates already scheduled for 1990, Bill still had the stellar support of Don Stover and Art Stamper. But he needed a good tenor harmony singer to enable him to do the kind of duets that he and Red had favored. When Pete Kuykendall recommended Jimmy Gaudreau, Bill was well aware of his music, but was skeptical of his ability to adapt to the old-time style. He thought of Gaudreau as a "progressive" musician who was most comfortable with jazz or rock style improvisations. But when Bill met Jimmy at the International Bluegrass Music Association's World of Bluegrass convention in Owensboro, Kentucky, in 1990, and played with him for a few hours in the Bluegrass Unlimited hospitality suite, he realized that their voices blended extremely well. He may not have known that while Jimmy was a master musician in several genres, he had in fact always loved the sound and repertoire of the Brother Duets and other old-time country acts. Gaudreau also took pride in his ability to adapt his phrasing and vocal timbre to the sound of virtually any lead musician with whom he worked.

Born in Wakefield, Rhode Island, on July 3, 1946, Gaudreau had begun his musical career as an electric guitarist and did not pick up a mandolin until he was sixteen years old. His mandolin style, in fact, was first adapted from guitar phrases. Since that time, though, he had worked with some of America's greatest bluegrass musicians, including the Country Gentlemen and Bela Fleck, and he continued to play with other groups during his tenure with Bill Clifton. Very soon after their first meeting in Owensboro, Jimmy met with Bill and Don in Bristol, Virginia, and recorded an album called *Where the Rainbow Finds Its End* (Elf 102), the second item produced for Bill's newly formed label. Gaudreau accompanied Bill on a trip to England in 1992, playing principally in the folk clubs. Jimmy was humbled by the chance to play with someone of Bill's historic stature but was particularly thrilled to get the chance to travel to England. While there, Jimmy made important contacts that enabled him to book future trips to that country.[27]

Bill lost his other steadfast musical partners with the death of Don Stover on November 11, 1996,[28] and the death of Art Stamper on January 23, 2005.[29] Bill held fast to his musical dream, however, and fortunately continued to find musicians of Gaudreau's stature. He had also introduced, back in 1980, a new recording label that enabled him to do exactly the kind of songs he cherished, and in the style he favored. Bill had planned an autoharp tribute album for the County label, hoping that it would come out in 1981 to mark the one hundredth anniversary of Charles F. Zimmerman's invention. When David Freeman, proprietor of the County label, said that he could not make the deadline, Bill got the recordings back with a payment of $3,000, obtained from the sale of a bronze statue of a bull. Bill then organized his own label, Elf, in order to release the album on time. *Autoharp Centennial Celebration* (Elf 101), which was the very first Elf release, featured both Bill and Mike Seeger on the autoharp, and reunited Bill with John Duffey and Tom Gray. The word Elf, according to Bill, was a tribute to Tineke: elf is Dutch for *eleven*, meaning that Tineke was "more than a ten."

Except for the concert given in Coventry, England, in 1976 (heard on *Alive!*, the second CD in the series), the six Elf CDs document the last important phase of Bill's musical career, spanning the years 1991 to 2004. Although deaths had brought to an end the career of the First Generation, Bill continued to make music successfully with other musicians. In some instances he was billed, on recordings and concerts alike, as simply "Bill Clifton and Jimmy Gaudreau." Heeding the advice of Tineke, who noted that Bill was now selecting the best musicians he could find, by 2001 he had begun describing his band as "the Pick of the Crop." Art Stamper and Jimmy Gaudreau played occasionally with this band, but it also included such talented musicians as Jean-Blaise Rochat, Joost van Es (a classically trained Dutch violinist), old reliable Tom Gray, and Raymond W. McLain. Famed for his effervescent stage personality, McLain was a superb tenor harmony singer, a multi-instrumentalist, an educator who had played for many years with his family band from Berea, Kentucky, and a veteran of concerts played around the world. The McLain Family had made at least fourteen trips abroad, appearing in sixteen countries under the auspices of the State Department.[30] Pick of the Crop played infrequently but did make periodic visits to the European continent, playing at places like Rienk Janssen's Big Bear Festival in Zuidlaren, Holland. Sometimes when Bill was not present, these musicians performed and recorded as J. B.'s Band (headed by Jean-Blaise Rochat).[31]

The music played during the Elf years was no longer exclusively bluegrass but instead was a composite of mostly heartfelt, sentimental songs from an earlier era done with an old-time flavor. Fiddle, banjo, and autoharp instrumentals usually appeared in most concerts, but listeners more often heard beautiful, plaintive songs like "Mary Dear," "Little White Washed Chimney," "'Mid the Green Fields of Virginia" and other popular items from the Starday-Mercury years. Bill also reached back frequently into the songbags of his hillbilly heroes. While generally obscure to twenty-first-century listeners, such songs as the Blue Sky Boys' "The House Where We Were Wed" and "Beautiful," the Bailes Brothers' "Pretty Flowers" and "I Guess I'll Go On Dreaming," and the Sons of the Pioneers' "The Rainbow's End" were given sincere treatments that made them live again.

Bill and sisters (top: Ann and Fifi; bottom: Mary Lynn and Martha), late 1990s.
Courtesy of Mary Lynn Marburg Brett

Bill even managed an excellent and almost-exquisite Swiss-style yodel on "In My Dear Old Southern Home," a vocal tour de force that he employed too infrequently. The overall effect of this music was mellow, relaxed, and comforting, qualities that were far afield from the hard and driven bluegrass heard during the era, and significantly different from the music on Bill's early records. His response to a reviewer who had complained about the subdued nature of one of his CDs is instructive of Bill's frame of mind and musical approach during these years: "Faster and more hard-edged is no longer where I am in life."[32]

Bill's romance with old-time country music had never wavered in the long years of his career. Instead, it grew stronger over time, as the notes to some of his Elf albums reaffirmed. In the liner notes to *River of Memories* (Elf 103), a collection of religious and inspirational songs, described by Bill as his favorite recording, he argued that the songs were "reminiscent of the quiet, gentle years of the late nineteenth and early twentieth centuries." Bill's romanticism, and misconception of the sources of the music that he loved, had never been more strongly displayed. The songs *were* gentle; the times in which they first appeared were not. The songs originally had served as vehicles for dealing with, or escaping from, the insecurities of an era

that was anything but quiet and relaxed for millions of poor Americans—
a period of racial strife and violence, agricultural unrest, labor conflict,
poverty, and war.

As the 1990s gave way to a new century, Bill, now in his late seventies,
never totally abandoned his music but instead played only scattered and
special dates in the United States and Europe. He always managed to find
good musicians at festivals who were eager to play with him, although
they were not always familiar with the lyrics of his songs. For example,
at a party given for the legendary fiddler Tex Logan on April 25, 2012,
and preserved on YouTube, Bill did a creditable job on all four verses of
"'Mid the Green Fields of Virginia," while his backup singers struggled
to capture only an occasional word. While he had always expressed reluc-
tance to be identified as a bluegrass singer, Bill nevertheless maintained
his interest in the style, took a strong interest in its history and documentation, and maintained a warm relationship with its musicians. He continued
to attend the annual meetings of the IBMA and participated in efforts to
commemorate the contributions made by older musicians. Meanwhile,
Bill's own distinctive contributions began to be recognized. In 1981 his
version of "Mary Dear" had been included in the *Smithsonian Collection
of Classic Country Music*, a box set of 144 of country music's most important recordings. In 1990 he was named the first honorary president of the
newly formed British Bluegrass Music Association and was honored by
America's Society for the Preservation of Bluegrass Music (SPGMA) and
by the IBMA (a Distinguished Achievement Award in 1992 and selection
to the Hall of Fame on October 2, 2008). He participated in a television
series, "Grassroots to Bluegrass," hosted by Mac Wiseman. Recorded on
eight DVDs (each over an hour in length), the series featured about thirty
musicians, including such bluegrass people as the Osborne Brothers, Jesse
McReynolds, and Kenny Baker, along with a variety of other old-timers
like Janette Carter, Walter Bailes, Brother Oswald (Beecher Kirby), John
Hartford, and Charlie Louvin, who reminisced about their experiences and
sang some of their favorite songs. Bill performed two songs—"Give Me the
Roses Now" (with Mike Seeger contributing autoharp accompaniment and
tenor harmony) and "Little White Washed Chimney" (with Mac Wiseman
singing on the chorus).

While his occasional concerts and awards were highly prized, Bill probably gained his highest level of satisfaction from the realization that the
Carter Family and their music were receiving the tributes they deserved. He

himself had contributed immeasurably to that recognition, first with his loving tribute on Starday Records back in 1963. That album had won converts to the family's music both abroad and in the United States. In the United States Bill contributed to the preservation of the Carters' legacy through his collaboration with Janette Carter in Hilton, Virginia. A daughter of A. P. and Sara Carter, Janette had been honoring her father's request to present shows, first in A. P.'s store and then, after 1976, in a little hillside theater called the Carter Fold, located very near the store. Along with her brother Joe and sister Gladys, Janette Carter performed and co-hosted weekly programs there in the years that followed. The shows featured mostly local musicians but did occasionally attract big-time professional performers, such as Johnny Cash, Maybelle's son-in-law through his marriage to June Carter. Cash in fact presented one of the last performances of his life at the Fold, on July 5, 2003 (he died only a couple of months later).[33] On August 3 and 4, 2012, the Carter Fold, now managed by Janette's daughter, Rita Forrester, celebrated the eighty-fifth anniversary of the recordings made by the original Carter Family in Bristol, Tennessee, in August 1927. Bill Clifton proudly performed, both as a solo act and as a supporting musician for other acts.[34]

Bill was involved in virtually every formal tribute paid to the Carters. He served as a mentor to Dennis Cash, whom he described as the "leading proponent of Carter Family music" when Cash (no relation to Johnny) recorded two tribute albums to the Family: *Songs of Home* (West Station WSR122507) and *Sing Me a Carter Family Song* (Blue Circle BCR-034). Bill was quoted liberally in the Zwonitzer biography of the Carters and on the National Public Radio documentary of the Carter Family,[35] and was asked to give the induction remarks in 2001 when the Carters were named to the Bluegrass Hall of Honor. Although he could not persuade the Virginia legislature to adopt the Carters' "Longing for Old Virginia"[36] as the state song, Bill did help frame the family's international recognition. Capitalizing on the seventy-fifth anniversary of the Bristol, Tennessee, sessions of August 1927, when the Victor Talking Machine Company first recorded the Carter Family and Jimmie Rodgers, Gary McDowell, director of the Institute of United States Studies at the University of London, sponsored "The Sunny Side of Life: The Carter Family and America's Music" on October 11–12, 2002, to commemorate the event. Bill presented his memories of the family in a slide-show lecture and hosted a panel of scholars, including Nolan Porterfield, Neil Rosenberg, and this author, who assessed the Carter Family's place in American music history from each of the participant's unique perspectives. The conference was capped off with a concert presented at the American ambassador's mansion, featuring Janette Carter (A. P.'s and Sara's daughter), Bill, and Mike Seeger. Dame Margaret Thatcher was only one of several dignitaries who attended.

With its link to Carter Family history, his house in Mendota continued to be an emotional refuge for Bill. Devastating floods on the Holston River, however, cast some doubts about the advisability of living in the region. The flood of March 2002 swept away much of Bill's papers and correspondence, including prized letters written to him by Woody Guthrie. Bill and Tineke almost suffered a much worse fate; they and their dog Pushkin were forced onto the second floor of their home by floodwaters. They used oil lamps and subsisted on peanut butter and crackers. Tineke, though, professed not to be too perturbed because, as a product of Holland, she was accustomed to floods. Laurel, who was attending Virginia Tech in Blacksburg, heard that the Holston was sweeping through her parents' first floor, and she took a quick trip to Mendota to see how they were coping with the disaster. She drove within two miles of her home, but floodwaters prevented her from completing the journey. So for the last couple of miles, she walked through mud and water along the railroad tracks. Her harrowing trip was chronicled in a local newspaper.[37]

Tineke may not have been overly discomfited by floods, but the loneliness of a semi-isolated life and the parochial nature of Southwest Virginia culture took their toll. In 2008 she and Bill purchased a home near Beckley, West Virginia. They did not sell the Mendota home, but since it was only a three-hour drive from Beckley, they kept it as a rural refuge for Bill. They were also comfortable with some of the local doctors they had met in Virginia and had found a church in Bristol (the Emmanuel Episcopal Church) whose minister they liked very much. After a temporary alienation from the church of his youth, Bill had returned to the Episcopal Church, finding solace in its comforting rituals and confident that it was now liberal enough in its attitude toward gays, women, and racial minorities to warrant acceptance.

Their new residence in West Virginia was a large lake house on Chatham Lake in Glade Springs, a gated community, just south of Beckley. Located in a heavily wooded area, with much wildlife, including eagles, the home offered a touch of ordered nature and solitude. The development was in some ways ill-suited for Bill. He had wanted to build a log cabin, but development rules would not permit such construction. There were four golf courses, but Bill did not play golf. Most of his neighbors were Republicans and, while Bill professed no political allegiance, he generally voted Democratic. He believes that he and Tineke were the only two people in the development who voted for President Obama. They have no close neighbors and are happy with the solitude, but they nevertheless find comradeship within the community whenever it is needed. An occasional trip to the golf clubhouse provided a good meal and an opportunity to have social discourse with their neighbors.

Now in almost complete retirement, Bill had ample opportunity to reflect on his long and varied career. Occasionally, media recognition made the music public aware of the contributions that he had made to the world of bluegrass and old-time music. On November 10, 2012, for example, internationally renowned radio announcer Eddie Stubbs played Bill's version of "Lonely Heart Blues" on his WSM radio show and waxed eloquently about Bill's role in the popularization of the music abroad. While Bill could take great pride in the many awards that came to him in the waning years of his career, he could only have reservations or mixed feelings about some of the personal and private consequences of his ambition and passionate absorption in his work. His children, for the most part, had built successful careers, and in a few cases exhibited the direct positive impact of Bill's own career preferences in their lives. Grainger, for example, noted on his website that a childhood of travel and residence in foreign lands, and a stint in the Peace Corps, had underscored and supported his work as an educator and philanthropist.[38] Charles ("Tad"), on the other hand, had always enjoyed accompanying his father on his music tours and helping out at the record table and any other way he could. He had worked hard in several capacities at the Luray Festival, had traveled with his dad during the Country Gentlemen days, and had been part of the British tours made by Bill Monroe in 1966 and 1975. This childhood exposure to show business may have been an anticipation of and preparation for his adult work as a consultant to the film industry in Hollywood. After all, he had already had his own intimate exposure to superstars, in his childhood relationship with people like Bill Monroe, Carter Stanley, and John Duffey.[39]

If Bill had hoped for musical careers by his children, his desires, for the most part, were not fulfilled. Several of his children, such as Grainger and Cameron, did toy with musical performance to the point of taking violin, piano, or dance lessons, but only two of them, Chandler and Laurel, invested a great amount of time in music. Along with her career in children's education (as director at the Sundrops Montessori school in Charleston, South Carolina—a product in large part of her family's commitment to Waldorf education), Chandler also performed professionally as a mandolin, guitar, and fiddle player in bluegrass and Celtic bands, while also booking groups in local coffeehouses.[40] Bill's youngest child, Laurel, tried unsuccessfully to grasp the intricacies of country fiddling—although she was proud of the fiddle that Art Stamper gave her. She loved and respected her father but frankly could not develop much affection for country music. However, she did demonstrate her awareness and understanding of music in other ways. She became a world-class collector and advocate of African popular and traditional styles of music. For several years she hosted a radio show, "African Voices," which was broadcast at separate times in Blacksburg and Seattle.[41]

Despite the success exhibited by some of his children, Bill's family was fractured, a reality far removed from the familial harmony that his nostalgic songs described and revered. He has been quick to admit that he

Bill singing to his stepdaughter, Flory Gout (2001). Courtesy of Bill Clifton

was not always a good husband or father, and that an emotional distance has marred his relationship with a few of his children. He has no contact at all with some of them. Like Mike Seeger, Bill had too often found greater comradeship among his fellow musicians than with his family and was not always available when they needed his fatherly attention or understanding. Some of the children, though, seem deeply pained when they hear Bill assert that he was not a good father. His stepdaughter Flory Gout, for example, speaks of him as "a loving stepfather, kind and gentle and soft spoken," and recalls a warm, affectionate, and thoughtful person who always remembered the special milestones of childhood and loved spending quality time with his grandchildren when they came to the lake.[42] Chandler, Flory, and Laurel all cherish intimate memories of their childhood when Bill awakened them for school with a cup of tea and some warm caressing words, or when he celebrated their birthdays, Christmas, or other special occasions with flowers or a little song. Traditional celebrations were very important to Bill. He liked nothing more than huddling around the fireside with his kids on Christmas Eve, smoking his pipe, listening to recorded holiday songs, or reading Dickens's *A Christmas Carol*.

Bill's extended family of musicians, both abroad and in the United States, would be surprised to hear any accounts of estrangement between him and other people. The memory and respect for his music have remained undiminished in those distant climes where he was once active. It is only fitting that one of his earliest musical disciples in England, Rick Townend—an alumnus of the Echo Mountain Boys—has maintained perhaps the strongest loyalty to his mentor. In 2012 Townend organized a trio, the Kent Carters, to commemorate and preserve the musical legacy of the Carter Family. Performing Carter Family songs in the original trio style, complete with guitar and autoharp accompaniment, Townend, Jane Richards, and Gill Sands (playing the parts of A. P., Sara, and Maybelle, respectively) demonstrated the ways in which Carter Family music had insinuated itself into the British folk music scene. Their performances, of course, also paid tribute to the man who had done most to make the Carters' music respectable in Britain, and they in fact paid homage to him in a CD called *A Tribute to Bill Clifton*. The album included a variety of songs earlier recorded by Bill, plus a song written by a local fan, Chris Lidyard, called "Bill Clifton is Playing the Greyhound Tonight."[43]

Bill hasn't played the Greyhound, or any other folk club, in close to forty years, but many fans can still remember those heady days back in the

Bill with a favorite autoharp, made by Tom Morgan (1990s). Courtesy of Bill Clifton

mid-sixties when he was picking and singing in them four or five times a week. He can be justly proud of the role that he played in making people in England and Europe conscious of American bluegrass and old-time music, a contribution echoed by his later work in Australia, New Zealand, and Japan. England's Echo Mountain Boys are only a few of the musicians abroad who profited directly from Bill's encouragement and tutelage. Bill's contributions, though, began well before he relocated in England, through his work in the United States as a musician, promoter, and song collector. Bill's famous songbook served as an essential source for many of the young musicians of the sixties who got caught up in the folk music revival. As a self-described song carrier, Bill won satisfaction in hearing many of these beloved songs performed around the world.

Song carrier that he has been, Bill Clifton's contributions are more than those of a tasteful collector, promoter, and distributor, for he was an even better interpreter of songs. With his sincere, signature baritone warmth and his skill at surrounding his vocals with the instrumental work of the best musicians of his time, Bill breathed new life into these cherished songs. We all are beneficiaries of his lifetime of devotion to the music he loved.

NOTES AND SOURCES

Bill Clifton's recordings are out of print except for *The Early Years, 1957–1958* (Rounder 1021), a compilation of his most important Starday recordings; *Bill Clifton and the Hamilton County Bluegrass Band* (British Academy of Country Music BACM D418), an album first recorded in New Zealand; and the impressive box collection, *From Poor Valley to the World* (Bear BCD-16425), produced in Germany and released on June 13, 2001. Containing eight CDs with 358 songs and tunes, the Bear collection spans the years from 1954 to 1991. Otherwise, Bill's recordings can frequently be found on Amazon, iTunes, and other websites. His musical performances can also be found on an extensive number of YouTube sites, including segments of shows given at festivals.

This biography has relied heavily on oral interviews, email messages, and other written material obtained from Bill Clifton, his family, and friends who knew him on a personal basis or who made music with him. The bulk of my information came from an extensive interview with Bill Clifton in Glade Springs, West Virginia, June 9, 2013, and from numerous telephone conversations and email correspondence conducted since that time. He has also provided occasional written reminiscences, including a remarkable "confession," titled "Money or the Lack Thereof."

A March 2002 flood from the Holston River in Southwest Virginia ruined much of Bill's business material and personal correspondence, including some letters from Woody Guthrie. However, I was able to consult quite a lot of magazines, music ephemera, and other printed material at his home in West Virginia. These included a large file cabinet of 3x5" cards listing recorded country songs that he had accumulated since his teenage years.

Conversations and emails with many of Bill's family members were very helpful, including his four sisters: Mary Lynn Brett, telephone, September 18 and 21, 2012, and August 10, 2015; Ann Hoffman, telephone, October 29, 2012; Fifi Peck, telephone, April 1, 2015; Martha Sadler, telephone, April 2, 2015; four of his children: Tad, telephone, June 1, 2014; Chandler, interview in Charleston, South Carolina, March 10, 2014, and emails, March 17, 2014, and June 7, 2015; Flory Gout, emails on September 1 and 20, 2013; and Laurel, telephone, April 11, 2015. Mary Lynn Brett also provided photographs of Bill's family.

I talked to Bill's wife, Tineke Marburg, by telephone on November 2, 2014. We also had informal chats during my visit to Glade Springs, West Virginia.

Bill's oldest living friend, Hamilton "Hap" Hackney, provided information about their childhood in a telephone conversation on December 20, 2013, in email correspondence, and in the form of a photograph of him and Bill as teenagers.

Indispensable published information includes Rienk Janssen's one-hundred-page hardcover book that accompanies *From Poor Valley to the World*, the major boxed collection of Bill's recordings produced by Richard Weize for the Bear label in Germany. Other highly valuable sources are the unpublished "Bill Clifton Interviews," conducted by Bert Nobbe, Kees Jansen, and Harry Vogel (Nieuwe Pekela, October 30, 2004, and Winterswijk, November 27, 2004); Richard Spottswood, "An Interview with Bill Clifton," ran in successive issues of *Bluegrass Unlimited* 2, nos. 9–11 (March, April, and May 1968); Joe Ross, "Bill Clifton: Preserving the Old Songs," *Bluegrass Unlimited* 28, no. 1 (July 1993), 36, 44; the short biography found in Fred Bartenstein, Gary Reid, and others, *The Bluegrass Hall of Fame: Inductee Biographies, 1991–2014* (Louisville, Kentucky: Holland Brown, 2015); and a "Business Resume" (unpublished), prepared by Bill Clifton after the completion of his master's degree in business, 1957.

Billboard magazine frequently ran items on Bill Clifton during his commercial career, beginning as early as his radio broadcasts in Virginia in 1951. *Billboard* occasionally also included personal information, including the births of some of his children.

The Mudcat Café folk music website was very helpful on several occasions, providing recording data and information about songs and singers. Subscribers, who consisted of both musicians and fans, communicated frequently about songs, performers, and recordings.

Ronald D. Cohen has been a prolific historian and publisher of material dealing with the American Folk Music Revival. See especially *Rainbow Quest: Folk Music and American Society, 1940–1970* (Amherst: University of Massachusetts Press, 2002). For Great Britain, see Michael Brocken, *The British Folk Revival:1944–2002* (Hants, England: Ashgate, 2003).

Neil Rosenberg, *Bluegrass: A History* (Urbana: University of Illinois Press, 1985), is the most comprehensive treatment of this musical phenomenon. But much has happened in the decades since the book was published, so it needs a serious revision.

Nathan Gibson, *The Starday Story: The House That Country Music Built* (Jackson: University Press of Mississippi, 2011), is an indispensable study of the influential record company that recorded Bill Clifton's most important songs, as well as the record producer, Don Pierce, who was highly influential in Clifton's career.

Mark Zwonitzer, with Charles Hirshberg, has provided the best available biographical study of the Carter Family: *Will You Miss Me When I'm Gone? The Carter Family and Their Legacy in American Music* (New York: Simon and Schuster, 2002).

Barry Mazor tells us much about the ways in which country music became commercial, by discussing the life and career of the man who first recorded the Carter Family and Jimmie Rodgers: *Ralph Peer and the Making of Popular Roots Music* (Chicago: Chicago Roots, 2015).

NOTES TO THE INTRODUCTION

1. Jim Huey reminded me of some of the details concerning our 1976 trip to the Red Fox Inn and the Indian Springs Festival, in a telephone conversation from Cincinnati, April 24, 2015.

2. Pat Flory recalled the trip in an essay for *Bluegrass Unlimited*, while also remembering his friendship with Bela Fleck: Donna Glee Williams, "Bela Fleck and Pat Flory: A Lot of Water under the Bridge," *Bluegrass Unlimited*, vol. 27, no. 2 (August 1992), 28–36.

3. Eleanor Ellis talks briefly about her decision to move to Washington, D.C., after the Red Fox Inn gig: see http://www.eleanorellis.com/cd.htm.

4. I talked to Dennis Cash by telephone, on May 23, 2015.

NOTES TO CHAPTER 1, "DISCOVERING COUNTRY MUSIC"

1. In addition to the information provided by Bill Clifton and his sisters, I learned something about his family background from scattered printed sources. Some information on his father, Grainger Marburg, came from St. Paul's Alumni magazine, *Alumni Horae* 68, no. 3 (1988): 142; obituaries, 69. In an interview with Richard Spottswood, Bill said that he was born at home on the kitchen table, and he suggested that his maternal grandfather may have been the attending physician: see "An Interview with Bill Clifton," *Bluegrass Unlimited* 2, no. 9 (March 1967): 3.

2. For Bill's mother, father, and grandfather, see https://www.myheritage.com/search-records?action=person&siteId=67675642&indId=1000008&origin=profile; an obituary of Mary R. Marburg appeared in the *Baltimore Sun*, November 2, 2000.

3. Brief references to William and George Hemming Hocking are found in the Bolitho family links website: http://members.iinet.net.au/~bob.bolitho/stjust5/47117 .html. Bill's maternal ancestors, the Bolitho family, take their name from a village in western Cornwall, England.

4. Brief references to Bill's Marburg forebears are found in Clayton Colman Hall, *Baltimore: A Biography* (Lewis Historical Publishing, 1912), 507.

5. Calvert information is briefly outlined at the school's website, http://www .calvertschoolmd.org/Page/About/history (2014).

6. Carol Sorgen presents a brief description of Selsed in "An English Country Manor," *Chesapeake Home*, September 18, 2006.

7. Bill's reference to "the little farm" came in an interview with the California Bluegrass Association on November 11, 2009.

8. For the *Old Dominion Barn Dance* and Sunshine Sue Workman, see Harry Kollatz Jr., "Barn Stormer," *Richmond Magazine* (September 15, 2014); and Caroline Morris, *The Voice of Virginia: WRVA and Conversations of a Modern South* (Williamsburg, Va.: College of William and Mary, 2012).

9. Guy Logsdon, from Tulsa, Oklahoma, is a librarian, author, musician, and authority on Western Swing, cowboy music, and Woody Guthrie. Jean Ann Boyd conducted an extensive interview with him, "Oral Memoirs of Guy Logsdon," for the Baylor University Institute for Oral History, Waco, Texas (July 11, 2003), available at http://contentdm.baylor.edu/cdm/ref/collection/buioh/id/6180.

10. For a discussion of the romantic appeal exerted by Appalachia, see Bill C. Malone, "Appalachian Music and American Popular Culture: The Romance That Will Not Die," in *Appalachian Heritage* 22 (June 1994): 66–77. Readers, though, might be interested in a book that combines two of country music's most hoary myths, Celticism and Appalachia, as presumed sources of the music: Fiona Ritchie and Doug Orr, *The Musical Voyage from Scotland and Ulster to Appalachia* (Chapel Hill: University of North Carolina Press, 2014).

11. Nat Hentoff, *Listen to the Stories: Nat Hentoff on Jazz and Country Music* (Boston, Mass.: Da Capo, 1995).

12. Bill told interviewer Richard Spottswood that he was four or five years old when he heard a professional accordion player perform at a party for "maybe 500

kids": Spottswood, "An Interview with Bill Clifton," *Bluegrass Unlimited* 2, no. 9 (March 1967), 3.

13. Bob Pinson wrote a good short essay on the M. M. Cole Publishing Company for Paul Kingsbury, ed. *The Encyclopedia of Country Music* (New York: Oxford, 1998), 319; a lengthy description of *Country Song Roundup*, covering its first fifteen years of existence (1949–1963), is available at http://www.hillbilly-music.com/publications/story/index.php?pub=9010.

14. A brief history of Baltimore's Hippodrome Theater is found on the France-Merrick Performing Arts Center site: http://www.france-merrickpac.com/index.php/history.

15. In a 2009 interview for the California Bluegrass Association, Bill speculated about the migration of rural people to Baltimore, saying that as a youth he heard a lot of music played by people who "came from depressed areas of southwest Virginia, eastern Kentucky, western North Carolina and settled in Baltimore." See http://www.cbaontheweb.org/hook.aspx?hookid=1110.

16. Henry Glassie, Clifford R. Murphy, and Douglas Dowling Peach have written an outstanding book about Ola Belle Reed, the singer and five-string banjoist who did much to preserve traditional music in the Upper South. The book is a good introduction to the music heard at the country music parks: *Ola Belle Reed and Southern Mountain Music on the Mason-Dixon Line* (Atlanta: Dust-to-Digital, 2015). The book is packaged with a two-CD set of Ola Belle's music.

17. John Fahey, the legendary roots guitarist, is largely tongue-in-cheek in his blurb, "How Bluegrass Music Destroyed My Life," but he has some important insights about the reasons he and many of his youthful friends in the Washington, D.C., area embraced bluegrass music. He also reaffirms the important role played by Don Owens and WARL. For more on Fahey, see Eddie Dean, "In Memory of Blind Thomas of Old Takoma, John Fahey, 1939–2001," *Washington City Paper* (March 9–15, 2001), available at http://www.washingtoncitypaper.com/special/fahey030901.html. In an interview with Ian Nagoski for *Sound American*, Dick Spottswood talks about how he and other Washington, D.C., youth such as Pete Kuykendall, John Duffey, Tom Gray, and Bill Emerson discovered bluegrass. He says, "We all just grabbed onto hillbilly music like it was a life raft" (see http://soundamerican.org/ian-nagoski-interviews-dick-spottswood). Spottswood is also profiled in Tovin Lapan, "Obsession for the Old and Obsolete," *Naples (Florida) Daily News*, March 10, 2006, available at http://www.naplesnews.com/community/obsession-for-the-old-and-obsolete-ep-406649635-331470981.html.

18. An obituary for Judge H. Hamilton Hackney is found in *Alumni Horae* 41, no. 1, p. 48 (obits 2) (originally published Spring 1961), available at http://archives.sps.edu/common/text.asp?Img=6327.

19. Shamus Rahman Khan, a graduate of St. Paul's, has written a provocative book on his alma mater: *Privilege: The Making of an Adolescent Elite at St. Paul's School* (Princeton, N.J.: Princeton University Press, 2011).

20. Interview with Hap Hackney, December 20, 2013.

21. Although he did not complete his education at St. Paul's, "William Augustus Marburg" is listed in Alan Hall's "Notable Paulies," found in *Alumni Horae* 77, no. 1 (Spring 1977): 34, article 11. He is listed as a 1949 graduate and is described as "Bill Clifton, Bluegrass Musician." In an email on December 7, 2013, Bill Clifton said that St. Paul's periodically invited him to reunions and asked him for money. His reply was that if he "chose to donate to any school, it would be the Adirondack-Florida school, my alma mater."

22. A brief discussion of Gilman School can be found at https://books.google.com/books?id=8bEAAAAAYAAJ&pg=PA34&dq=gilman+school,+baltimore&lr=&ei =eBrhSenXJYPcygTYh6maDQ&hl=en#v=onepage&q=gilman%20school%2C%20 baltimore&f=false.

23. Edward Palmer Lincoln was interviewed by Marian Ludlow on March 3, 1987, for the University of Florida Oral History Program: see http://ufdc.ufl.edu/UF00006072/ 00001/8j?search=marian+%3dludlow. In a thirty-seven-page transcript, he gives a very brief version of the Mexico trip (on p. 7) but concentrates only on the Acapulco robbery and the automobile wreck. He makes no mention of Bill's country music interest or career.

24. An account of the death in Mexico of Bill's uncle, Theodore Marburg Jr., is in Chris Dickson, *Americans at War in Foreign Forces: A History, 1914–1945* (Jefferson, N.C.: McFarland, 2014), 75.

25. The best account of the *Grand Ole Opry* is Charles Wolfe, *A Good Natured Riot: The Birth of the* Grand Ole Opry (Nashville: Vanderbilt University Press and the Country Music Foundation Press, 1999).

26. The best introduction to the Bailes Brothers' sound at that period of their career is the CD *Oh So Many Years* (Bear 15973).

27. Some information about the Florida-Adirondacks High School is found in Blythe Grossberg, "A Profile of the Ransom Everglades School in Florida," available at http://privateschool.about.com/od/miam1/a/A-Profile-Of-The-Ransom-Everglades -School-In-Florida.htm.

28. Bill Ramsey provides some recollections of Bill Marburg's days at Florida-Adirondacks in his notes to the album *Wanderin'* (Hillbilly Records HR 5001).

NOTES TO CHAPTER 2, "FROM THE UNIVERSITY OF VIRGINIA TO THE STARDAY YEARS"

1. For a good overview of the history of the University of Virginia, see Virginius Dabney, *Mr. Jefferson's University: A History* (Charlottesville: University of Virginia Press, 1981).

2. The context for Bill's University of Virginia experience is touched upon in Richard Guy Wilson and Sara A. Butler, *University of Virginia: The Campus Guide* (Princeton, N.J.: Princeton Architectural, 1998); see also Coy Barefoot, "Down on the Corner," *University of Virginia Magazine*, Spring 2007, available at http://uva magazine.org/articles/down_on_the_corner.

3. Joe Palumbo's obituary was in *The Daily Progress*, Charlottesville, Virginia (May 30, 2015).

4. The St. Elmo Club of the University of Virginia is described at http://aig.alumni.virginia.edu/elmo/history.

5. The relationship between Bill Clifton and Paul Clayton is discussed in Bob Coltman's fine book, *Paul Clayton and the Folksong Revival* (New York: Scarecrow, 2008). Henry Glassie provided a recollection of Clayton in Glassie, Murphy, and Peach, *Ola Belle Reed*, 135–37. See also Catherine Moore, "The Song Collector: How Folksinger Paul Clayton Brought the Music of Virginia to the World," *University of Virginia Magazine*: Spring 2010, available at http://uvamagazine.org/articles/the_song_collector.

6. Clifton's and Clayton's 1952 recordings that were intended for the Stinson label were reissued in 1975 by the Bear Family label in Germany: *A Bluegrass Session, 1952* (Bear BFX 15001).

7. Inspired by the recent Spanish-American War, "I'll Be There, Mary Dear" was written in 1902 by the Tin Pan Alley composers, Andrew Sterling (lyrics) and Harry Von Tilzer (music). The song was recorded as early as 1902 by the minstrel singer Byron G. Harlan, in the 1920s by Richard Harold, Roy Harvey, and Charlie Poole, and in 1940 by Gene Autry. The recording history of this and other "hillbilly" songs is chronicled in Tony Russell's indispensable collection, *Country Music Records: A Discography, 1921–1942* (New York: Oxford University Press, 2004).

8. Nathan Gibson talks about Bill's choice of the name "Clifton" in *The Starday Story: The House That Country Music Built* (Jackson: University Press of Mississippi, 2011), 90.

9. *Billboard*, March 31, 1951, p. 85.

10. Brief accounts of Roy Hall can be found in Charles K. Wolfe, *Classic Country: Legends of Country Music* (New York: Routledge, 2001), 134–35, and on the *Oldies* website—see "Roy Hall biography" at http:www.oldies.com/artist-biography/Roy-Hall.html.

11. Some information on Bob Miller is found at the Nashville Songwriters Hall of Fame website: http://nashvillesongwritersfoundation.com.s164288.gridserver.com/Site/inductee?entry_id=2509.

12. Good biographies of Woody Guthrie include Joe Klein, *Woody Guthrie: A Biography* (New York: Knopf, 1980) and Ed Cray, *Ramblin' Man: The Life and Times of Woody Guthrie* (New York: Norton, 2004).

13. Mark Zwonitzer, with Charles Hirshberg, *Will You Miss Me When I'm Gone? The Carter Family and their Legacy in American Music* (New York: Simon and Schuster, 2002).

14. In 2014 Bear Family issued a five-CD box set of the Chuck Wagon Gang including all of their Columbia recordings issued from 1936 to 1955 (Bear BCD 17348).

15. The best historical survey of bluegrass has been written by Neil Rosenberg: *Bluegrass: A History* (Urbana: University of Illinois Press, 1985).

16. A short profile of Johnny Clark was printed in the "Questions and Answers" section of *Bluegrass Unlimited* 27, no. 3 (September 1992): 11–12.

17. Ivan Tribe, *Mountaineer Jamboree: Country Music in West Virginia* (Lexington: University Press of Kentucky, 1985).

18. Bill's résumé, prepared by him after his graduation for help in seeking employment, contains pertinent information concerning his degrees and graduation dates.

19. Some information on the Blue Ridge label can be found at "Cataloger's Corner: Bluegrass on Blue Ridge Records" (July 11, 2014) on the blog *Field Trip South: Exploring the Southern Folklife Collection*, available at http://blogs.lib.unc.edu/sfc/index.php/2014/07/11/catalogers-corner-bluegrass-on-blue-ridge-records.

20. Two of George Shuffler's most important "disciples" left nice remembrances of their teacher: "Tom Gray on George Shuffler," *Bluegrass Today*, April 8, 2014, available at http://bluegrasstoday.com/tom-gray-on-george-shuffler; and "James Alan Shelton Remembers George Shuffler," in *Bluegrass Today*, April 7, 2014, available at http://bluegrasstoday.com/james-alan-shelton-remembers-george-shuffler. Shuffler endearingly demonstrates his cross-picking style of guitar playing on a brilliant excerpt from *Flatpicking Guitar Magazine*'s instructional DVD "Clinch Mountain Guitar," November 20, 2006: available at https://www.youtube.com/watch?v=BTr9xudLyCY. See also the discussion of Shuffler in Bartenstein, Reid, and others, *Bluegrass Hall of Fame*.

21. H. Conway Gandy, "Don Owens: The Washington, DC Connection," *Bluegrass Unlimited* 22, no. 5 (November 1987): 68–72.

22. Peter Goldsmith, *Making People's Music: Moe Asch and Folkways Records* (Washington, D.C.: Smithsonian Institution Press, 1998).

23. For discussions of Mike Seeger, see Bill C. Malone, *Music from the True Vine: Mike Seeger's Life and Musical Journey* (Chapel Hill: University of North Carolina Press, 2011); Hazel Dickens and Bill C. Malone, *Working Girl Blues: The Life and Music of Hazel Dickens* (Urbana: University of Illinois Press, 2008); and Ray Allen, *Gone to the Country: The New Lost City Ramblers and the Folk Music Revival* (Urbana: University of Illinois Press, 2010).

24. Connie B. Gay merits a book-length survey. When one is written, it will profit from a lengthy interview with him conducted by Douglas B. Green for the Country Music Hall of Fame and Museum in Nashville. In the meantime, good synopses of his career include: Joe Sasfy, "The Hick from Lizard Lick," *Journal of Country Music* 12, no. 1 (1987): 16–24, 33; Patrick Kiger, "When Washington Was Nashville North," on *Boundary Stones: WETA's Local History Blog*, http://blogs.weta.org/boundary stones/2014/04/03/when-washington-was-nashville-north; and "Connie B. Gay in Caswell, North Carolina," on the blog of the Caswell County Historical Association: http://ncccha.blogspot.com/2007/05/connie-b-gay-in-caswell-county-north.html (May 8, 2007).

25. Ralph Stanley's autobiography, written with Eddie Dean, *Man of Constant Sorrow: My Life and Times* (New York: Gotham, 2009), is an invaluable, though opinionated, account of the Stanley Brothers' personal history and of the development of bluegrass. Unfortunately, the book has no index. Gary Reid has compiled an excellent account of the Stanley Brothers' recordings: *The Music of the Stanley Brothers* (Urbana: University of Illinois Press, 2015).

26. Too often ignored or forgotten, Carter Stanley received a fine tribute from Eddie Dean: "Carter Stanley: The Sibling That 'O Brother' Forgot," in the *Wash-*

ington Post, May 23, 2004, available at http://washingtonpost.com/wp-dyn/articles/A45463-2004May21.html.

27. Don Pierce is the subject of a one-hour-and-fifty-three-minute interview in the Oral History Collection at the Country Music Hall of Fame in Nashville (May 3, 1974).

28. Nathan Gibson, in *The Starday Story* (written with the assistance of Don Pierce), discusses Pierce, as well as Bill Clifton's association with the label. The book also includes an exhaustive listing of Starday recordings, both singles and LPs.

29. Charles Wolfe has written a good account of Tommy Jackson in *Devil's Box: Masters of Southern Fiddling* (Nashville: Vanderbilt University Press, 1997), 186–96. One of the best accounts that I've seen for Gordon Terry is the obituary written for the *Decatur (Georgia) Daily News*, April 10, 2006. The family of Roy M. "Junior" Huskey has maintained a blog about him: http://juniorhuskey.com.

30. Starday's inauguration of its "packaged goods program" was mentioned by Bill Sachs in his *Billboard* column, "Folk Talent and Tunes" (August 17, 1959). Bill Clifton's Starday recordings are listed in David Edwards, Mike Callahan, and Patrice Eyries, "Starday Album Discography," parts 1 and 2, http://www.bsnpubs.com/starday/stardaystory.html, and at http://www.rocky-52.net/chanteursc/clifton_bill.htm.

31. For the American folk music revival, see Ronald C. Cohen, *Rainbow Quest: Folk Music and American Society, 1940–1970* (Amherst: University of Massachusetts Press, 2002); Neil Rosenberg, ed., *Transforming Tradition: Folk Music Revivals Examined* (Urbana: University of Illinois Press, 1993); and Israel Young, with Scott Baretta, *The Conscience of the Folk Revival: The Writings of Israel "Izzy" Young* (Lanham, Md.: Scarecrow, 2013).

32. Tad Marburg's comments about his maternal grandparents came in a telephone interview with him, from Los Angeles, November 2, 2012.

33. Dixie Deen was born Iris May Lawrence in Sutton Coldfield, England. Richard Thompson wrote an excellent remembrance in "Dixie Hall Remembered," *Bluegrass Today*, February 2, 2015, available at bluegrasstoday.com/dixie-hall-remembered. Nancy Cardwell wrote an earlier appreciation: "Dixie Hall," *Bluegrass Unlimited*, November 1, 2013, available at bluegrassmusic.com/content/2013/feature/dixie-hall. I profited also from an undated article by Deen in the British magazine *Country and Western Express* (early 1961), provided by Robert Ronald.

34. Bill Clifton's visit to A. P. Carter during his final hospital stay is described in Zwonitzer, *Will You Miss Me?* 331.

35. *Little Sandy Review* 24 (March–April 1964): 10.

36. *Mudcat Café*, July 31, 2008, in a thread titled RE: The Death of Louis Collins.

37. Neil V. Rosenberg, "The Springhill Mine Disaster Songs: Class, Memory, and Persistence in Canadian Folksong," in *Northeast Folklore: Essays in Honor of Edward D. Ives*, edited by Pauleena MacDougall and David Taylor (Orono: University of Maine Press, 1959), 153–87.

38. Thomas A. Adler's purview is much larger than the title of his book: *Bean Blossom: The Brown County Jamboree and Bill Monroe's Bluegrass Festivals* (Urbana: University of Illinois Press, 2011). The question of "the first" bluegrass festival

has been addressed by several writers: Joe Ross, for example, explores the role played by Don Owens in the Yahoo! discussion group "So Just What Is Bluegrass Music?" available at https://groups.yahoo.com/neo/groups/nwbluegrass/info, which features Ross's treatment of the two rival festivals in a post titled "Don Owens' and Bill Clifton's Bluegrass Days" (https://groups.yahoo.com/neo/groups/nwbluegrass/conversations/topics/24485). "Welcome to Historic Watermelon Park" is a brief account of the one-day event held there on August 14, 1960. http://watermelonpark.com/about-us. Bill's work at Oak Leaf Park in Luray, and a schedule of events there, were announced in *Billboard* on June 26, 1961. Published accounts of the Luray controversy include Rosenberg, *Bluegrass* 179–80, and Richard D. Smith, *"Can't You Hear Me Calling": The Life of Bill Monroe* (Boston: Little, Brown, 2000).

39. Ronald D. Cohen provides some information on George Wein and Newport in *A History of Folk Music Festivals in the United States: Feasts of Celebration* (Lanham, Md.: Scarecrow, 2008), 84, and in his larger book, *Rainbow Quest: The Folk Music Revival and American Society, 1940–1970* (Amherst: University of Massachusetts Press, 2002).

40. Profiles of Pete Kuykendall, John Duffey, Tom Gray, Eddie Adcock, Don Stover, and other IBMA inductees can be found in Bartenstein, Reid, and others, *Bluegrass Hall of Fame*. I conducted a telephone interview with Pete Kuykendall on November 5, 2014. Otherwise, see Bartenstein and Reid, and others, *Bluegrass Hall of Fame*. For John Duffey, see Bartenstein and Reid, and others, *Bluegrass Hall of Fame*, and, especially, *Congressional Record* 143, no. 2 (January 9, 1997), which contains remarks by Congressman David R. Obey; see also detailed obituaries of Duffey from the *Washington Post*, *Bluegrass Unlimited*, and *Sing Out*! I gained information on Tom Gray through a telephone interview with him on January 9, 2015, and from a short biography on his high school website: http://westernhighschool-dc.org/gray_t.html. Gray talked about his indebtedness to George Shuffler at http://bluegrasstoday.com/tom-gray-on-george-shuffler. I talked to Eddie Adcock, by telephone on January 15, 2015. We can learn a lot about the emerging bluegrass scene in the Washington, D.C., area in an article about Tom Morgan, a musician and luthier who was there to view it all, and who made major contributions as a musician and instrument maker: see Reni Haley, "Best of Both Worlds," *Bluegrass Unlimited* 23, no. 2 (August 1988), 19–22. See also Gibson, *Starday Story*, 88–89, on the early role played by Buzz Busby, Scotty Stoneman, and Jack Clement in the making of the Washington, D.C., bluegrass scene. For the Baltimore bluegrass community, see Tim Newby, *Bluegrass in Baltimore: The Hard Drivin' Sound and Its Legacy* (Jefferson, N.C.: McFarland, 2015); Geoffrey Himes, "From the Hills: How Mid-Century Migrants from the Mountains Brought Bluegrass—and More—to Baltimore," *City Paper*, January 12, 2000; and Geoffrey Himes, "Forgotten Gardens: From Ashe County, North Carolina, to Baltimore's Hillbilly Ghettoes, Musicians Planted the Seeds for New Grass and the Old-time Music Revival," *City Paper of Baltimore*, October 21, 2015, available at http://www.CityPaper.com/news/features/himes-folk-music-20151021-story.html.

41. Karen L. Cox has discussed the romantic appeal of the South felt by American songwriters in *Dreaming of Dixie: How the South was Created in American Popular Culture* (Chapel Hill: University of North Carolina Press, 2011).

42. My information concerning Bill's popularity in England before his residence there, as well as his high polling in country music magazines in that country, came from clippings provided by Robert Ronald (received on August 12, 2015).

NOTES TO CHAPTER 3, "TAKING OLD-TIME MUSIC TO ENGLAND"

1. Tony Russell shared his fine (but unpublished) essay, "'Rough but Strikingly Melodious': British Responses to American Country Music in the 1930s"; email, September 3, 2012.

2. Despite the impressive contributions made by Carson Robison to country music—in both the United States and England—there is no definitive biography of him. Bruce Elder provides a brief description of his career, "About Carson Robison," at http:www.cmt.com/artists/carson-robison/biography. Patrick Huber has also given a good account of Robison's activities in the early days of country music in "The New York Sound: Citybilly Recording Artists and the Creation of Hillbilly Music," *Journal of American Folklore*, 127, no. 504 (Spring 2014): 140–58. A prospective biographer would certainly profit from the underutilized material in the Carson J. Robison Collection at the Leonard H. Axe Library, Pittsburg State College, Pittsburg, Kansas.

3. John Szwed, *Alan Lomax: The Man Who Recorded the World* (New York: Viking, 2010); E. David Gregory, "Lomax in London: Alan Lomax, the BBC and the Folk-Song Revival in England, 1950–1958," *Folk Music Journal* 8, no. 2 (2002): 136–69. Alan Lomax and Peggy Seeger, *American Folk Guitar* (London: Robbins Music, 1957), contained instructions on how to play fifteen traditional songs.

4. Hank Reineke, *Ramblin' Jack Elliott: The Never-Ending Highway* (Lanham, Md.: Scarecrow, 2010).

5. Skiffle music and history can be found on *Washboards, Kazoos, Banjos: The History of Skiffle* (Bear BCD 16099), a six-CD set of 176 tracks, and an accompanying hardcover book, 2014. See also Groper Odson, "The History of Skiffle," *Freight Trains, Last Trains, and Rock Island Lines* (October 10, 2012), available at http://www.rockhistory.co.uk/rockhistory-cd-the-history-of-skiffle.

6. Mike Paris: "Notes on Country Music in Britain" (unpublished), sent to me in an email, September 8, 2013. John Atkins: "Finding the Carter Family in the UK," unpublished essay; telephone interview with Atkins, December 27, 2014. Dave Barnes: emails, December 21 and 22, 2014; Martin Hawkins, "The Story of the British Archive of Country Music," *Journal of Country Music*, available at http://country-music-archive.com/dave-barnes. Jim Marshall: telephone interview, June 26, 2014; short interview on the web with Jim Marshall, January 5, 2015, available at http://thefolkvoice.com/2015/01/08/jim-marshall-5th-January-2015. Rick Townend: telephone interview, December 26, 2014; emails, September 1, 2012, and January 15, 2015; "Rick Townend-Musician," available at http://www.ricktownend.co.uk./CV.htm; and "Rick Townend and Bill Clifton," available at http://www.ricktownend.co.uk/Rick-BillClifton.htm. Gavin Gaughan wrote an obituary of Murray Kash in *The Guardian*, June 17, 2009, available at http://theguardian.com/music/2009/jun/18/obituary-murray-kash.

Robert Ronald has been extremely helpful to me in the preparation of this biography, first in a telephone interview on June 8, 2015, and since that time by providing me with photocopies of Bill Clifton's activities noted in English magazines. For example, he painstakingly photocopied items dealing with Clifton's record reissues and early appearances in England originally printed in *Country and Western Express* during the period 1958 to 1963.

7. A good profile of the Sevenoaks school can be found in *The Good Schools Guide* (London) at http://www.goodschoolsguide.co.uk/school.

8. *Billboard* announced Bill's arrival in England on December 7, 1963, p. 12, and told about his affiliation with the Patrick Robinson Agency on December 21, 1963.

9. Jason Heller reviewed eighteen songs about the Beatles, but errs, I believe, in suggesting that "Beatle Crazy" was an anti-Beatles song. It should instead be viewed as a novelty that was inspired by the singers' incredible popularity: see www.avclub.com/article/the-beatles-just-got-to-go-18-anti-beatles-songs-75625.

10. Vic Smith reminisces about Jim Marshall, Mike Story and *Folk Voice* at "The Mudcat Café," mudcat.org/thread.cfm?threadid=130199. In a letter to me, dated January 23, 2013, Bill Clifton said that he knew of eighty-four hour-long editions of *Folk Voice*, beginning in 1958, that were deposited in the Southern Collection at UNC-Chapel Hill.

11. J. P. Bean, *Singing from the Floor: A History of British Folk Clubs* (London: Faber and Faber, 2014).

12. Laurence Diehl comments on Bill Clifton's guitar playing in an interview from August 2011, conducted by Paul Roberts: http://www.banjocrazy.com/articles/diehl_1.shtml.

13. Brian Bull's comments were made on a folk music blog, February 2, 2015: http://rhylfolkclub.com/2015/02/04/memories-of-the-60s.

14. Bill's tribute to Tom Morgan's skill as an autoharp builder was made in discussions with me and in a newsletter, the *Autoharp Clearinghouse* (February 1991).

15. Rick Townend provides a good summary of the Echo Mountain Boys: http://www.ricktownend.co.uk/EMB.htm. For an overview of the British bluegrass scene, see Joe Ross, "Great Britain: Great Bluegrass," *Bluegrass Unlimited* 25, no. 10 (April 1991).

16. For the Keele Folk Festival, see Victor Keegan, "From the Archive: Money No Object at Festival of Pure Folk." Originally published July 17, 1965, in *The Guardian*. Available at http://www.the guardian.com/the guardian/2009/jul/17/folk-festival -dylan.

17. The Cambridge Folk Festival is profiled in "History of Cambridge Folk Festival," http://www.cambridgefolkfestival.org/history-of-cambridge. A listing of performers who appeared at the festival from 1965 through 2014 can be found at https://cambridgelivetrust.co.uk/folk-festival/history/past-artists.

18. The Royal Albert Hall concert: a program brochure is reproduced at http://itsthedubliners.com/ref_prog_1965_fcp.htm.

19. Bill Clifton recalled Mike Seeger's first trip to England, and discussed how the experience broadened him, in Richard Thompson, "Mike Seeger Remembered,"

Bluegrass Today, August 26, 2009, available at http://bluegrasstoday.com/mike -seeger-remembered. See also Bill C. Malone, *Music from the True Vine*, 116–17.

20. Tom Morgan discussed his important role as a luthier, supplying instruments to both Bill Clifton and the Townend brothers, in a telephone interview with me, January 12, 2015.

21. For John Cohen's remarks, see Allen, *Gone to the Country*, 171 and 172.

22. The Stanley Brothers 1966 tour of England is described by David W. Johnson, *Lonesome Melodies: The Lives and Music of the Stanley Brothers* (Jackson: University Press of Mississippi, 2014), 229. Ralph Rinzler wrote one of the first academic accounts of Bill Monroe in his essay for Bill C. Malone and Judith McCulloh, eds., *Stars of Country Music* (Urbana: University of Illinois, 1976); Jim Rooney also held an excellent interview with the bluegrass king, published in *Bossmen: Bill Monroe and Muddy Waters* (New York: Dial, 1971). There is now a small but growing library of books devoted to Monroe. Richard Smith's *Can't You Hear Me Callin'* is probably the best. Dave Cousins and Ian McCann's recollections of Bill Monroe's 1966 tour of England are described in J. P. Bean, *Singing from the Floor: A History of British Folk Clubs* (London: Faber and Faber, 2014).

23. Pete Kuykendall spoke of his trip to Germany in a telephone interview with me, November 5, 2014.

24. Bill Ramsey, notes to *Wanderin'* (Hillbilly Records HR 5001); for more on Bill Ramsey, see his website, http://www.ramsey.de/bio-english.html.

25. Garth Gibson, notes to Bill's New Zealand record, *Two Shades of Bluegrass* (Kiwi SLC 93), re-released on an English label, BACM (D418). Paul Trenwith sent me an informative email on June 6, 2015, and a more extensive essay on July 12, 2015.

26. Hamilton County Bluegrass Band website: www.hamiltoncounty.co.nz; see also Daniel C. Gore, "Paul and Colleen Trenwith," *Bluegrass Unlimited* 24, no. 1 (July 1989): 23–28.

NOTES TO CHAPTER 4, "A RENEWED COMMITMENT TO FULL-TIME MUSIC"

1. Bill Clifton talked about his dealings with the Atlantic Trust Bank in St. Peterport, on the Channel Island of Guernsey, in an unpublished essay written for me, "Money or the Lack Thereof." He referred to the owner of the bank, Allen J. Lefferdink, as "one of the 20th Century's greatest con artists." For further information on Lefferdink, see John F. Berry, "Far-Flung Financial Empire Ends in Collapse," *Watertown Daily Times*, April 28, 1976, p. 4.

2. Ewan MacColl's dismay at "the overwhelming American influence on the English folk song revival" is discussed in *Sing Out!* 9, no. 3 (Winter 1959–1960), 9. Information on MacColl can be found many places, including Working Class Movement Library (WCML)—see http://www.wcml.org.uk/maccoll/biography—and in the biography written by Ben Harker, *Class Act: The Cultural and Political Life of Ewan MacColl* (London: Pluto, 2007).

3. One of the most accessible introductions to A. L. Lloyd is the interview conducted by Mark Gregory, September 20, 1970, available at the Mustrad website:

http://www.mustrad.org.uk/articles//lloyd.htm. Less available, but outstanding, is the interview with Lloyd in 1951 conducted by Alan Lomax: see the American Folklore Society Oral History Project, Archive of Folk Culture, American Folklife Center, Library of Congress, Washington, D.C.

4. J. P. Bean comments on the left-wing leanings of the British folk music revival in *Singing from the Floor*, 2.

5. In an email message to me, September 1, 2012, Rick Townend said that Ewan MacColl and Peggy Seeger's Singers Club in London was "in many ways directly responsible for the decline in interest for anything American in the folk clubs." Mike Paris and John Atkins both told me about the fairly widespread English suspicions concerning the Peace Corp's alleged complicity with the CIA.

6. Information on Christine Marburg and her Danish diplomat husband can be found at various websites, including *Memim Encyclopedia*: http://memim.com/tjarda-van-starkenborgh-stachouwer.html.

7. Some information on Cor and Margaret Sanne, and *Country Gazette*, is available at the CMS Productions website: http://www.cms-country.nl/engels/historie-e.htm.

8. Some of my information on Richard Weize came from a telephone interview I conducted with him on July 2, 2013; other useful sources include Dick Spottswood, "Bear Family: Doing It Right," *Bluegrass Unlimited* 28, no. 9 (March 1994), 42–47; and Jim Bessman, "Bear Family Nurtures Quality Boxed Sets," *Billboard*, March 13, 2004.

9. *Carl T. Sprague—The First Popular Singing Cowboy* was issued as an LP on the Bear Family label (BF 150002) in 1978.

10. Bill's recording of "Waltzing with Bears" can be heard on *From Poor Valley to the World* and on some Bear Family anthologies. The song seems to have been inspired by a song or poem from Dr. Seuss, "My Uncle Terwilliger Waltzes with Bears" in *The Cat in the Hat Songbook* (1967), but it was composed in its current and very different form by Dale Marxen. The Mudcat Café website has a good discussion of the song's origins at the Mudcat.org thread "Origin: Waltzing with Bears—the Mudcat Café," October 14, 1999.

11. The *Der Musikladen* YouTube segment can be found listed under the name of Alexis Korner.

12. For information on Hedy West, I found useful Irwin Silber, "You're Hedy West," *Sing Out!* 14, no. 4 (September 1964): 29–32; and Derek Schofield, obituary, *The Guardian*, September 11, 2005, available at http://www.theguardian.com/news/2005/sep/12/guardianobituaries.artsobituaries1.

13. Bobby Bare recorded the song, with some of his own lyrics, as "500 Miles Away from Home" (RCA 8238), August 24, 1963.

14. Hedy West's comments about the "velvet" nature of Bill's singing were made on September 18, 2000, on the Mudcat Café website, http://mudcat.org/thread.cfm?threadid=9584.

15. Hoathly Hill: see Christian Thal-Jantzen, "A Short History of Hoathly Hill," at http://www.hoathlyhilltrust.org.uk/about/about-the-community, and Christopher Middleton, "Why Can't the British Live Together?" *The Telegraph*, January 27, 2001,

available at http://www.telegraph.co.uk/property/4812729/why-can't-the-British
-live-together.html.

16. The Waldorf Education site contains an explanatory section titled "Why Waldorf Works," available at https://waldorfeducation.org/waldorf_education. There are many biographies of Rudolf Steiner. Two of the most useful are: the entry in *Encyclopedia of World Biography*, available at http://www.notablebiographies.com/supp/Supplement-Sp-Z/Steiner-Rudolf.html; and John Lanigan, "Rudolf Steiner: An Introduction to His Life and Work by Gary Lachman," in *Philosophy Now: A Magazine of Ideas* (April/May 2015), available at https://philosophynow.org/issues/68/Rudolf_Steiner_An_Introduction_to_his_life_and_work_by_Gary_Lachman.

17. John Atkins conducted an interesting interview with Red Rector (late 1981); the text is available at http://www.mandolin.myzen.co.uk/rector.html.

18. I talked with David Freeman by telephone on January 13, 2015; Marshall Wyatt's interview with Freeman was published as "Every County Has Its Own Personality." An interview with David Freeman, in *The Old-Time Herald* 7, nol. 2 (Winter 1999–2000); Richard Thompson also interviewed Freeman: "Dave Freeman Remembers," *Bluegrass Today*, February 17, 2008, available at http://bluegrasstoday.com/dave-freeman-remembers. Some information on Don Larkin can be found at the Hillbilly.com website: www.hillbilly-music.com/dj/story/index.php?id=16631.

19. Charles Faurot's contributions were best explained in a National Public Radio documentary, "Historic Recordings Tell Clawhammer Banjo History," March 21, 2006, available at http://www.npr.org/templates/story/story.php?storyId=5293105. There are numerous obituaries of Charles Faurot; one of the most informative is Ellen Robertson, "Charlie Faurot," *Richmond Times-Dispatch*, August 29, 2013, available at http://www.richmond.com/obituaries/featured/article_a8dba8ea-4ab7-557d-b32a-d6989ed9efcd.html.

20. Some of the best recollections and obituaries of Joe Wilson appeared on the Mudcat Café website, May 19, 2015. These include a reprint of an excellent obituary by Ralph Berrier Jr. in the *Roanoke Times*, May 18, 2015. Quote is from Richard Spottswood, "A Bluegrass Experiment: The First Generation," *Bluegrass Unlimited*, August 1978, 22–27.

21. Bill Monroe's visit to Scotland is mentioned in his *European Tour '75 Souvenir Program: Bill Monroe and His Bluegrass Boys*, compiled by John Atkins and Bill Clifton, and in Jim Hyndman, "The Night Bill Monroe Came Home" (February 2003) at http://www.longway.pwp.blueyonder.co.uk/Page3.htm; see also Bob Black, *Come Hither to Go Yonder: Playing Bluegrass with Bill Monroe* (Urbana: University of Illinois Press, 2005).

22. Sab "Watanabe" Inoue provided invaluable information on the Japanese bluegrass scene, along with recollections of Bill Clifton's contributions there, in a lengthy email, September 1, 2015. He recalled that Michio Higashi had been one of the first Japanese musicians to receive a Bill Clifton tape from Don Pierce. For further information on bluegrass music in Japan, I read Eugene Chadbourne's biographical profile of the Japanese band Bluegrass 45 on http://www.allmusic.com/artist/bluegrass-45-mn0000067607. Stephanie P. Ledgin described the impact of Bluegrass 45 in

the United States: see *Homegrown Music: Discovering Bluegrass* (Westport, Conn.: Greenwood, 2004), 92. John Lawless also commented on Bluegrass 45's tour of the United States in 1971 and described the Bean Blossom festival, which featured both Bluegrass 45 and New Zealand's Hamilton County Band, as "the first international bluegrass festival": see http://bluegrasstoday.com/bluegrass-45-reunion-tour-in-japan.

23. Tineke Marburg telephone interview, November 2, 2014. The Lukas Community website is at http://lukascommunity.org/what_is.htm.

24. Tineke's work as a craftsman and as a volunteer at the Crisis Center in Bristol was mentioned on the blog, "Mimirock at Castle Yonder," http://mimirock-castleyonder .blogspot.com/2010/08/bill-clifton-longing-for-old-virginia.html.

25. Rick Lang discussed Rienk Janssen in "Promoter Rienk Janssen: The Holland Connection," *Bluegrass Unlimited* 24, no. 1 (July 1989): 76–79. I received a lengthy email message from Janssen; he mentioned the *Strictly Country* Farewell Reunion Festival, May 6–7, 2011, honoring Rienk Janssen (see *The European Bluegrass Blog*, April 10, 2011, at http://blog.ebma.org/2011/04/strictly-country-farewell-reunion_20 .html); and his notes to Clifton, *Around the World to Poor Valley* (Bear Family).

26. A twelve-page account of the Gusto Records litigation can be read at http:// openjurist.org/852/f2d/1287/clifton-v-gusto-records-inc.

27. I conducted a telephone interview with Jimmy Gaudreau, January 15, 2015. See also a seventeen-page interview with Gaudreau: http://www.mandozine.com/ media/CGOW/jimmygaudreau.html, and Marty Godbey's "Spectrum," *Bluegrass Unlimited* 15, no. 16 (December 1980): 14–21.

28. A short profile of Don Stover can be found at Bartenstein, Reid, and others, *Bluegrass Hall of Fame.* Kerry K. Hay wrote an obituary, "Don Stover's Funeral," available at https://groups.google.com/forum/#!topic/bit.listserv.bgrass-l/ObHoZ_cCvxU.

29. For Art Stamper, see Jon Weisberger's obituary in *No Depression* (magazine) 56 (March-April 2005).

30. Stephanie P. Ledgin, "On the Road and Off: Talking with the McLain Family Band," *Pickin'* 4, no. 6 (July 1977): 6–19. Raymond W. McLain is director of the Traditional Music Center at Morehead State University in Kentucky. Examples of his fine musicianship (banjo, fiddle, and mandolin) and tenor harmony are found on Bill Clifton and the Pick of the Crop, *Playing Where the Grass Is Greener* (Elf 105), and *JB's Band*, two discs (JBCD 01-02).

31. Jean-Blaise Rochat, email, from Prangins, Switzerland, February 14, 2013; an unsigned half-page biography is available at http://jbrbanjo.wordpress.com/ biography. For examples of European performance of bluegrass, see *10 Years of the European World of Bluegrass* (Strictly Country SCDR-66), a double CD of forty-eight bands from fifteen countries (including Bill Clifton and Pick of the Crop), recorded over a ten-year period prior to 2008 at the annual European World of Bluegrass Festival in Voorthuizen, Holland. Dave Freeman talked about his association with Charles Newman, Rodney McElrea, and *Country News and Views* in our interview of January 13, 2015.

32. Bill's letter to *Bluegrass Unlimited*, explaining that "faster and more hard-edged is no longer where I am in life's cycle," was in the issue of May 9, 2005.

33. Johnny Cash, YouTube of his appearance at the Carter Fold, July 5, 2003, at https://www.youtube.com/watch?v=exqGbd7EP2Q.

34. The Carter Fold website is http://www.carterfamilyfold.org; see also Janette Carter, "38th Carter Fold Festival," *Cybergrass: The Bluegrass Music News Network* (July 28, 2012), available at www.cybergrass.com/node/1547.

35. A full transcript of the PBS documentary, "The Carter Family: Will the Circle Be Unbroken," *The American Experience*, is found at http://www.pbs.org/wgbh/amex/carterfamily/filmmore/pt.html.

36. "I'm Longing for Old Virginia and You" was written by Joe Lyons (words) and E. Clinton Keithley (music), and was published in 1915 by Frank K. Root in Chicago. Probably intended as a barbershop quartet piece, the song was recorded by the Carter Family in 1934. Interestingly, the song began with a line from one of Bill Clifton's favorite songs, "Mid the Green Fields of Virginia," another "Carter Family Song," written in 1892 by the Tin Pan Alley composer Charles K. Harris. Bill can be seen and heard doing "Longing for Old Virginia" at the Executive Inn in Owensboro, Kentucky, June 2006. See the YouTube recording posted by Tammy Sheridan at https://www.youtube.com/watch?v=2tlyOc0RULU.

37. "Student Wades Her Way Home to Make Sure Parents Are Safe," *Bristol Herald Courier*, March 21, 2002, http://articles.dailypress.com/2002-03-21/news/0203210242_1_flood-bill-marburg-swollen.

38. Grainger Marburg received a B.A. from Hampshire College and an Ed.M. from Harvard. After twenty years of experience in education, philanthropy, and nonprofit management he was named CEO, in May 2014, of a nonprofit educational foundation, RAFT (Resource Area for Teaching). RAFT served twelve thousand educators each year who taught over nine hundred thousand students. Reported on the RAFT website, http://www.raft.net/news/blog/2014/05/ceo.

39. Charles "Tad" Marburg, a postproduction and distribution executive, received the John A. Bonner Medal of Commendation, from the Academy of Motion Pictures and Sciences on February 15, 2014, in Beverly Hills, California. In an announcement of the award, he was commended for his "cross-functional approach to filmmaking, bringing together artists and scientists in order to develop and share beautiful and captivating stories with audiences around the globe." Kerry MacLaine, "Forget the A-Listers: Oscars' Sci & Tech 2014 Honorees Deserve Spotlight," http://appealingstudio.com/forget-the-a-listers-oscars-scitech-2014-honorees-deserve-spotlight.

40. Chandler Marburg received dance and music training at the Boston Conservatory and taught dance for many years in New Hampshire. In 1993 she opened a Montessori school in Charleston, South Carolina, but continued to perform music actively, primarily as a singer and fiddler. I also interviewed her in Charleston, South Carolina, on March 10, 2014, and received a helpful email from her on March 17, 2014.

41. Laurel Marburg received her education at Central Washington University and Virginia Tech, majoring in biology and psychology. She had multiple interests, including long-distance running and African-derived music, but she was focused primarily on animal rights and welfare. She conducted research in Africa on at least

three occasions. I interviewed her on April 11, 2015; see also a short profile of Trintje Laurel Marburg, http://crossfitblacksburg.com/blog/athlete-profile-laurel-marburg.

42. Flory Gout has been extremely helpful to me, through a short unpublished essay titled "Biography of Bill Clifton: Growing Up with Bill as My Stepfather" (September 1, 2012), and a lengthy email, September 20, 2012. Married to a KLM pilot, Flory devotes much of her time to the cause of women's empowerment, as a self-described "birth doula" and "death doula," helping women through two critical passages in life's cycle.

43. The European Bluegrass Music Association website provides evidence of the widespread popularity of the music on the Continent. For example, see http://www.ebma.org. See also "There is a lot of bluegrass in Europe too," on the Mandolin Café Forum, March 15, 2007, available at http://www.mandolincafe.com/forum/archive/index.php/t-29999.html. A brief description of Rick Townend's Carter Family tribute group is "The Kent Carters," http://www.ricktownend.co.uk/KentCarters.htm.

DISCOGRAPHY (LPS AND CDS)

Although Bill Clifton recorded as early as 1952, when he was a student at the University of Virginia, examples of his work did not appear on an album until 1960, when Starday released *Mountain Folk Songs*. The songs heard on this album were those that had exhibited considerable popularity on 45s and 78s. Clifton seems not to have entered a studio with the specific goal of recording an album of new material until March 1961, when he produced his historic *Carter Family Memorial Album*. Earlier, Clifton had typically recorded four to six songs at a session. It is not always easy to determine with precision the identities of accompanying musicians who appeared on his early albums, because they frequently moved in and out of sessions. Richard Weize and others, though, have compiled a comprehensive listing of Bill Clifton's lifetime recorded output on the website *Praguefrank's Country Music Discographies* (http://countrydiscography .blogspot.com). The website lists not only the personnel, dates, and songs at each session, it also provides the album release numbers where the songs can be found. One should be reminded, however, that virtually all of these albums are out of print and can only be found through diligent research on websites and other sources.

The discography that follows is not complete. For example, it does not include all of the reissues that appeared in America, England, Japan, and the European continent. It does, however, include the overwhelming bulk of Bill Clifton's recorded repertory.

Mountain Folk Songs (Starday SLP 111), LP, 1960. Also called *Folk Songs from the Hills* on some reissues. Made up of previously recorded 45s and 78s from the Mercury and Starday labels, including the first recordings of "Little White Washed Chimney," "Mary Dear," and "Blue Ridge Mountain Blues." These songs remained central to Clifton's repertoire for the rest of his long career. Bill Clifton, vocal/ guitar; Johnny Clark, vocal/banjo; John Duffey, vocal/mandolin; Curley Lambert, mandolin; Ralph Stanley, banjo; Tommy Jackson, Benny Martin, Gordon Terry, Carl Nelson, Cal Newman, Sonny Mead, Bill Wiltshire, fiddles; George Shuffler, bass; Roy Self, bass; Mike Seeger, autoharp. Along with the Carter Family tribute, this was probably Clifton's most widely circulated and influential album. It won adherents for his music, and for bluegrass, in the United States, England, and Japan.

Carter Family Memorial Album (Starday SLP 146), LP, recorded in Nashville and Washington, D.C., March and April 1961. Bill Clifton, vocal/guitar; Smiley Hobbs, vocal/banjo; Mike Seeger, vocal/banjo/guitar/autoharp; Thomas Lee "Tommy" Jackson, fiddle; Norman Keith "Buddy" Spicher, fiddle; Roy M. "Junior" Huskey, bass. On the Washington, D.C., session, Johnny Clark, vocal/banjo; John Duffey, vocal/mandolin/dobro; Benny Martin, fiddle; and Roy Self, bass. Also released in Japan on the London label (GT 6003), this album contributed to the renewed popularity of the Carter Family in America and throughout the world.

Bluegrass Sound of Bill Clifton (Starday SLP 159). Issued in 1961, the LP consisted of cuts taken from recording sessions in Nashville, March 1958; Washington, D.C., August 1958; Nashville, November 1958; Washington, December 1958; and Washington, 1959.

Code of the Mountains (Starday SLP 271), LP, August 5–7, 1963. At this session Bill was joined, for the first time, by the full complement of Country Gentlemen: Charlie Waller, vocal/guitar; Eddie Adcock, vocal/banjo; John Duffey, vocal/ mandolin; and Tom Gray, vocal/bass. The sessions also included Mike Seeger, guitar/autoharp/banjo; and the twin fiddling of the Justice Brothers, Paul and Ray. This album was reissued in Japan in 1966 as *Bill Clifton Meets the Country Gentlemen* (London SLH 42).

Soldier, Sing Me a Song (Starday SLP 213), LP, Wynwood Studio, Falls Church, Virginia, September 1963. The songs included here paid tribute to Americans who fought in wars that ranged from the French and Indian War to the Korean War. Bill Clifton, vocal/guitar; John Duffey, vocal/mandolin; Paul Craft, vocal/ guitar/banjo; Curtis Lee and Carl Nelson, fiddles; Mike Seeger, autoharp/guitar; Tom Gray, bass.

Mountain Bluegrass Songs (Nashville NLP 2004), LP, 1964. A sampling of songs, including "Mary Dear," "Little White Washed Chimney," "Walkin' in My Sleep," "Flower Blooming in the Wildwood," and other war horses of his career, re-corded by Bill Clifton at earlier Mercury and Starday sessions.

Wanderin' (Hillbilly Records HRS 001), LP, September 18, 1964. Fourteen songs recorded by Bill Clifton, with his own guitar and autoharp accompaniment, at a private party in Basel, Switzerland.

Bluegrass in the American Tradition (Nashville NLP 2018), LP, recorded in Falls Church, Virginia on September 3–4, 1963, and released in 1965. Bill Clifton with the Country Gentlemen, plus the Justice Brothers (Paul and Roy) and Mike Seeger. Although the album included the bluegrass classic "Bringing Mary Home," the song apparently first reached the market through an independent recording by John Duffey and the Country Gentlemen.

Getting Folk Out of the Country (Folk Variety FV 12008), LP, 1972; (Bear BF 15008), CD, 2010. Bill Clifton, vocal/guitar/autoharp; Hedy West, banjo; Andrew Townend, mandolin. The album also included a cameo appearance by Clifton's wife Sarah Lee and three of their daughters, LeeLee, Camie, and Chandler, joining in on the singing of "Angel Band."

Blue Ridge Mountain Blues (County 740), LP, September 1973. A compilation of previously recorded Starday singles, including the title cut, "Mary Dear, "Lonely Heart Blues," "Old Pal of Yesterday," and others. It was also released in England on the Westwood label (WRS 047).

Come by the Hills (County 751), LP, June 4–5, 1974. Bill Clifton,vocal/guitar; Red Rector, vocal/mandolin; Walter Hensley, banjo; Kenny Baker, fiddle; Tom Gray, bass.

Bluegrass Session, 1952 (Folk Variety FV 12004). Bill Clifton, vocal/mandolin/ guitar, and Paul Clayton, vocal/guitar, originally recorded these songs at the Department of Speech and Drama at the University of Virginia and at radio station WINA in 1952. Clifton and Clayton were backed on most of the songs by Dave Sadler (banjo) and Carl Boehm (bass). Johnny Clark added his banjo and tenor vocals to the mix on four songs recorded at WINA. The LP was issued in 1975 on Bear (BF 15001).

Going Back to Dixie (Bear BF 15000). Thirty-six songs on a double LP, recorded at Wynwood Studios, Falls Church, Virginia, in 1963; reissued on the Bear Family label in 1975. Bill Clifton, vocal/guitar; Eddie Adcock, vocal/banjo; John Duffey, vocal/mandolin; Tom Gray, bass; Mike Seeger, autoharp; Paul and Roy Justice, fiddles; Charlie Waller, bass vocals; Pete Roberts (Kuykendall), guitar; Alice Foster, guitar.

Are You from Dixie? (Bear BF 15013), an LP recorded in West Germany, March 7–8, 1976. Bill Clifton, vocal/guitar/autoharp and Red Rector, vocal/mandolin. Jean-Blaise Rochat provided some accompaniment on guitar.

Another Happy Day (County 758), an LP recorded in Roanoke, Virginia, July 15–16, 1976. Bill Clifton, vocal/guitar; Red Rector, vocal/mandolin; Billy Edwards, banjo; Tater Tate, fiddle; John Palmer, bass. The album was also released in England on the Breakdown label (001).

Clifton and Company (County 765), an LP recorded at Tom T. Hall's studio in Brentwood, Tennessee, September 13–15, 1976. Bill Clifton, vocal/guitar/ autoharp; Mike Auldridge, dobro; Jim Brock, fiddle; Charlie Collins, lead guitar; Bill Keith, banjo; Tom Gray, bass; Red Rector, mandolin/vocals.

The Early Years, 1957–1958 (Rounder 1021), CD, 1977. This CD included Clifton's most important and popular recordings from his early years, and contributed greatly to the reinvigoration of his career after he returned to the United States.

Autoharp Centennial Celebration (Elf 101), a CD recorded in Springfield, Virginia, October 21–23, 1980. Bill Clifton, autoharp; Tony Williamson, guitar;

Mike Auldridge, dobro; John Duffey, mandolin; Mike Seeger, autoharp; Tom Gray, bass.

Beatle Crazy (Bear BFP 15121), Picture Record LP, 1983 (some sources give a later date). Along with the title cut, the disc included "The Little Girl Dressed in Blue" and four songs that reflected the British folk revival.

Where the Rainbow Finds Its End (Elf 102). A CD recorded in Spring 1991 in Bristol, Virginia. Bill Clifton, vocal/guitar; Jimmy Gaudreau, vocal/mandolin; Don Stover, banjo; Art Stamper, fiddle; Benny Sims, fiddle; Tom Gray, bass.

River of Memories (Elf 103), an all-gospel CD, recorded in Bristol, Virginia, in 1994 by Bill Clifton, guitar; and Jimmy Gaudreau, mandolin. Consisting of such songs as "In the Garden," "Give Me the Roses While I Live," "Church in the Wildwood," "Whispering Hope," and "Who Will Sing for Me," Clifton said this was his favorite of all the albums he had made.

Alive! (Elf 104), CD, 2001. The twenty-two songs heard here were recorded at a live show presented by Bill Clifton and Red Rector at Coventry, England, March 1976. Clifton believed that this album showed Rector at the top of his game as a skilled and innovative mandolin player.

From Poor Valley to the World (Bear BCD 16425), eight CDs, 2001. An impressive and major compilation of 358 songs and tunes that spanned Clifton's recording career from 1954 to the 1990s.

Playing Where the Grass Is Greener (Elf CD 105), recorded live at the Big Bear Festival in Zuidlaren, Holland, June 4, 2001. Bill Clifton, vocals/guitar/autoharp; Raymond W. McLain, vocals/fiddle/mandolin/banjo; Joost Van Es, vocals/fiddle; Jean-Blaise Rochat, vocals/banjo/guitar; Tom Gray, vocals/bass.

Mountain Laurel (Elf 106), a CD recorded by Bill Clifton and Pick of the Crop on June 14–15, 2004. Bill Clifton, vocal/guitar; Jimmy Gaudreau, vocal/mandolin; Art Stamper, fiddle; Tom Gray, bass.

Two Shades of Bluegrass (Kiwi SLC-93), LP, 1971, recorded in Auckland, New Zealand, March 31 and April 1, 1970; later released as *Bill Clifton and the Hamilton County Bluegrass Band* (British Academy of Country Music BACM D 418), CD, 2014. Bill Clifton, vocal/guitar/autoharp; Alan Rhodes, guitar; Paul Trenwith, banjo; Dave Calder, mandolin; Colleen Trenwith, fiddle; Lyndsay Bedogni, bass.

INDEX

BILL C. MALONE is professor emeritus of history at Tulane University. His books include *Don't Get above Your Raisin': Country Music and the Southern Working Class* and *Country Music, U.S.A.*

MUSIC IN AMERICAN LIFE

Traveling the High Way Home: Ralph Stanley and the World of Traditional
Bluegrass Music *John Wright*
Carl Ruggles: Composer, Painter, and Storyteller *Marilyn Ziffrin*
Never without a Song: The Years and Songs of Jennie Devlin, 1865–1952
Katharine D. Newman
The Hank Snow Story *Hank Snow, with Jack Ownbey and Bob Burris*
Milton Brown and the Founding of Western Swing *Cary Ginell, with special
assistance from Roy Lee Brown*
Santiago de Murcia's "Códice Saldívar No. 4": A Treasury of Secular Guitar Music
from Baroque Mexico *Craig H. Russell*
The Sound of the Dove: Singing in Appalachian Primitive Baptist Churches
Beverly Bush Patterson
Heartland Excursions: Ethnomusicological Reflections on Schools of Music
Bruno Nettl
Doowop: The Chicago Scene *Robert Pruter*
Blue Rhythms: Six Lives in Rhythm and Blues *Chip Deffaa*
Shoshone Ghost Dance Religion: Poetry Songs and Great Basin Context
Judith Vander
Go Cat Go! Rockabilly Music and Its Makers *Craig Morrison*
'Twas Only an Irishman's Dream: The Image of Ireland and the Irish in American
Popular Song Lyrics, 1800–1920 *William H. A. Williams*
Democracy at the Opera: Music, Theater, and Culture in New York City, 1815–60
Karen Ahlquist
Fred Waring and the Pennsylvanians *Virginia Waring*
Woody, Cisco, and Me: Seamen Three in the Merchant Marine *Jim Longhi*
Behind the Burnt Cork Mask: Early Blackface Minstrelsy and Antebellum American
Popular Culture *William J. Mahar*
Going to Cincinnati: A History of the Blues in the Queen City *Steven C. Tracy*
Pistol Packin' Mama: Aunt Molly Jackson and the Politics of Folksong
Shelly Romalis
Sixties Rock: Garage, Psychedelic, and Other Satisfactions *Michael Hicks*
The Late Great Johnny Ace and the Transition from R&B to Rock 'n' Roll
James M. Salem
Tito Puente and the Making of Latin Music *Steven Loza*
Juilliard: A History *Andrea Olmstead*
Understanding Charles Seeger, Pioneer in American Musicology
Edited by Bell Yung and Helen Rees
Mountains of Music: West Virginia Traditional Music from *Goldenseal*
Edited by John Lilly
Alice Tully: An Intimate Portrait *Albert Fuller*
A Blues Life *Henry Townsend, as told to Bill Greensmith*
Long Steel Rail: The Railroad in American Folksong (2d ed.) *Norm Cohen*
The Golden Age of Gospel *Text by Horace Clarence Boyer;
photography by Lloyd Yearwood*
Aaron Copland: The Life and Work of an Uncommon Man *Howard Pollack*
Louis Moreau Gottschalk *S. Frederick Starr*
Race, Rock, and Elvis *Michael T. Bertrand*

The University of Illinois Press
is a founding member of the
Association of American University Presses.

Composed in 10.5/14 Times New Roman
with Phosphate display
by Lisa Connery
at the University of Illinois Press
Manufactured by Sheridan Books, Inc.

University of Illinois Press
1325 South Oak Street
Champaign, IL 61820-6903
www.press.uillinois.edu